STIRLING COUNCIL LIBRARIES

D0307034

ATLAS OF CONFLICTS

# WORLD WAR I

## Stewart Ross

FRANKLIN WATTS
LONDON•SYDNEY

STIRLING
COUNCIL
LIBRARIES

J940.3

Titles in this series:

**THE ARAB-ISRAELI CONFLICT**
**THE KOREAN WAR**
**THE VIETNAM WAR**
**WORLD WAR I**
**WORLD WAR II: EUROPE**
**WORLD WAR II: THE PACIFIC**

© 2004 Arcturus Publishing Ltd

Produced for Franklin Watts by Arcturus Publishing
Ltd, 26/27 Bickels Yard, 151-153 Bermondsey Street,
London SE1 3HA.

Series concept: Alex Woolf
Editor: Philip de Ste. Croix
Designer: Simon Borrough
Cartography: The Map Studio
Consultant: Paul Cornish, Imperial War Museum,
   London
Picture researcher: Thomas Mitchell

Published in the UK by Franklin Watts.

All rights reserved. No part of this publication may be
reproduced, stored in a retrieval system, or
transmitted, in any form or by any means without the
prior written permission of the publisher, nor be
otherwise circulated in any form of binding or cover
other than that in which it is published and without a
similar condition being imposed on the subsequent
purchaser.

A CIP catalogue record for this book is available from
the British Library.

ISBN 0 7496 5449 X

Printed and bound in Italy

Franklin Watts – the Watts Publishing Group, 96
Leonard Street, London EC2A 4XD.

Picture Acknowledgements:
All the photographs in this book were supplied by
Getty Images and are reproduced here with their
permission.

## ABOUT THE AUTHOR

The author, Stewart Ross, spent several years teaching
at a variety of institutions in Britain, the USA and
Asia, before becoming a full-time writer in 1991. Since
then he has published numerous books for children
and adults, including *Leaders of World War I* and *The
Technology of World War I* in Hodder Wayland's World
Wars series.

# CONTENTS

# CHAPTER 1:
# THE EUROPEAN WAR

Wilhelm II, emperor of Germany 1888-1918, proved unequal to the task of wisely governing his inherited empire.

Irregular Macedonian fighters guard a highway leading to Salonika during the First Balkan War, 1912.

**W**orld War I, fought between 1914 and 1918, was a vast conflict that involved most of the world's major powers. Two grand alliances confronted one another: Britain, France, Russia, Italy, the USA and others on one side, and Germany, Austria-Hungary, Turkey and Bulgaria on the other. The war was fought on land, at sea, and, for the first time, in the air. Advances in technology had produced powerful and deadly new weapons which changed the nature of warfare forever. It began in Europe. In 1871 the large and industrially developed German Empire had replaced France as the continent's major power. Needing support, France had reached an agreement ('entente') in 1904 with its old enemy Britain, which was also anxious about German ambitions.

For many years Britain had enjoyed good relations with most of the states that made up Germany. The British royal family were of German descent and related to the Emperor of Germany. By the 1900s, however, this traditional Anglo-German friendship was breaking down. The British feared that their enormous overseas empire, covering one quarter of the world's surface, was threatened by German ambitions in Africa and elsewhere. Secondly, there was serious industrial and commercial competition between the two empires. Thirdly, Britain saw the construction of a large German Navy as a direct threat to Britain's worldwide naval supremacy. By 1910 Britain and Germany were in an arms race as they tried to outdo one another in warship construction.

**THE BALKAN QUESTION** For centuries the Balkan peninsula in south-east Europe had been part of the Turkish Ottoman Empire. In the nineteenth century Turkish power declined and the Balkans divided into small, independent states. The most politically influential were Greece, Romania, Bulgaria, Bosnia, and, especially, Serbia. In 1912-3 the intense rivalry between the Balkan states flared into two wars.

The neighbouring Russian and Austro-Hungarian Empires competed with each other for influence among the Balkan states. In 1908, for example, the Russians were furious when the Austro-Hungarians annexed the provinces of Bosnia and Herzegovina.

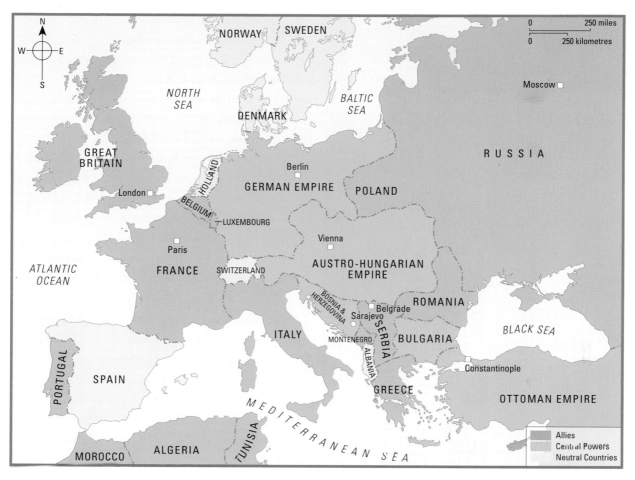

**A continent divided – how the states of Europe lined up to fight during World War I. Many had aligned with one side or another long before the fighting broke out in August 1914**

The chief bone of contention between them was Serbia, allied to Russia but distrusted by Austria-Hungary.

By 1914 Europe's dangerous international rivalries were backed up by a series of military alliances and agreements. On one side were the countries bound together by the Triple Entente (France, Britain and Russia) – the Allies. Ranged against them were the Central Powers of Germany and Austria-Hungary, linked by a Dual Alliance and supported with reservations by Italy (the Triple Alliance). Although

## MANPOWER OF THE MAIN EUROPEAN RIVALS

| Allies | | Population | Armed forces at outbreak of war |
|---|---|---|---|
| Triple Entente: | Russia | 167 million | 5 million |
| | France* | 39.6 million | 3.78 million |
| | Britain* | 46.4 million | 733,500 |
| **Central Powers** | | | |
| Dual Alliance: | Germany | 67 million | 4.5 million |
| | Austria-Hungary | 49.9 million | 3.35 million |
| Serbia (with Allies, 1914) | | 5 million | 460,000 |
| Italy (with Allies, from 1915) | | 35 million | 875,000 |
| Turkey (with Central Powers, 1914) | | 21.3 million | 300,000? |

* France and Britain could also draw on the considerable manpower of their overseas colonies.

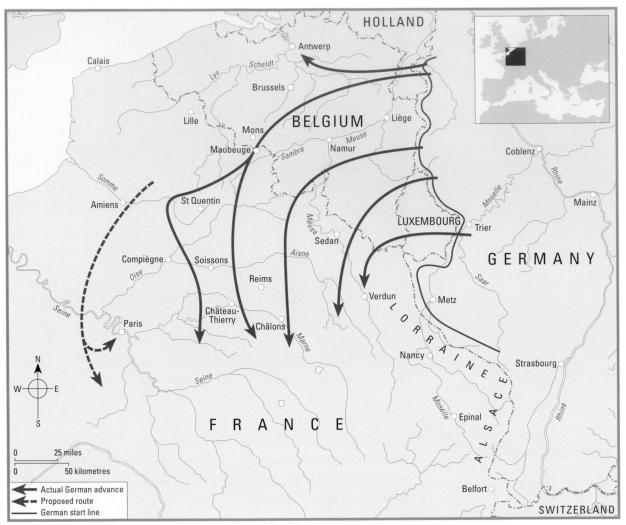

**Excellent on paper ... the German Schlieffen Plan envisaged a swift knock out blow in the west by driving through neutral Belgium and then surrounding Paris.**

these alliances were theoretically defensive, they meant a small conflict might well spread over the entire continent – and beyond.

**WAR PLANS** The outbreak of war in 1914 was not unexpected, and each side had made careful plans in advance. France, for instance, arranged to attack east into Alsace and Lorraine, provinces that Germany had seized in the war of 1870-1. Predicting such a move, in 1905 the German Chief of Staff General Count Alfred von Schlieffen had planned a swift attack on northern France through neutral Holland and Belgium. He believed this would quickly knock France out of the war and enable Germany to turn on Russia.

The Schlieffen Plan was altered, and weakened, by his successor, General Helmuth von Moltke. He reduced the force attacking from the north and by-

passed Holland. Nevertheless, Germany's assault on Belgium brought Britain into the war because it had guaranteed Belgian neutrality.

In the tense atmosphere of the early twentieth century, the European powers were terrified of being caught unawares. If one country increased the size of its armed forces, as Germany did in 1912, its rivals immediately did the same: Russia responded to Germany's 170,000 increase by swelling its army by half a million. This in turn frightened the Germans into further increases, so quickening the arms race. To meet these military requirements, all the major states except Britain obliged young men to undertake military service.

## THE ARMS RACE

Sir Edward Grey, Britain's foreign secretary at the outbreak of war, outlined the process of the arms race: *'One nation increases its army and makes strategic railways towards the frontiers of neighbouring countries. The second nation makes counter-strategic railways and increases its army in reply. The first nation says this is very unreasonable, because its own military preparations were only precautions, and points out ... that the first nation began the competition; and so it goes on, till the whole Continent is an armed camp covered by strategic railways.'*

[From *Twenty-five Years, 1892-1916*, Viscount E. Grey]

Helmuth von Moltke, the German commander whose failure to execute the Schlieffen Plan led to his dismissal in 1914.

The gigantic Russian army had the reputation of being a 'steamroller' – slow to get going but unstoppable once on the move. Furthermore, it was growing larger by the day, and Russia itself was developing mass-produced weapons. The German command feared that the longer war was delayed, the less chance they had of winning. Consequently, when Austria-Hungary threatened war with Serbia in July 1914, the German Emperor Wilhelm II gave his ally his full backing: if war was to come, his generals argued, then the sooner the better.

**INTO BATTLE** The outbreak of war was sparked by the assassination of Archduke Franz Ferdinand, heir to the throne of Austria-Hungary, on 28 June 1914. The Austro-Hungarians blamed Serbian terrorists for

Britain's iron shield: headed by the battleship HMS *Neptune*, the Royal Navy displays its power at the 1911 Spithead Fleet Review.

the outrage, and declared war on Serbia on 28 July. This started a domino effect. When Russia prepared to help Serbia, Germany declared war on it (1 August). France, Russia's ally, mobilized its troops so Germany declared war on it too. This launched the Schlieffen Plan, bringing Britain into the conflict (4 August). The Schlieffen Plan very nearly succeeded. The

Germans drove back the French in the east and moved through Belgium to within 50 km of Paris by late August. The French, with British support, halted the offensive on the River Marne, ending German hopes of a swift victory.

The Battle of the Marne, 5-9 September 1914, was the first in which aircraft played a vital role. The Schlieffen Plan called for the German armies to encircle Paris from the west. However, finding his enemy in disarray, the commander of the German First Army, General Alexander von Kluck, advanced across the Marne to the east of the capital. This was spotted by Allied aircraft. The French commander, Marshal Joseph Joffre, responded with an attack on Kluck's unguarded right flank – and the Germans were obliged to withdraw.

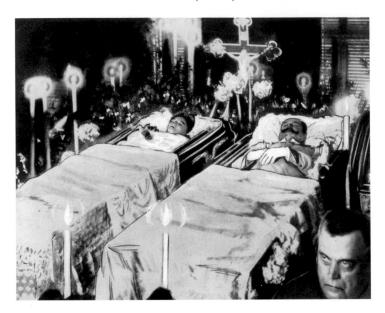

**Two deaths that led to millions more ... the bodies of the Austrian Archduke Franz Ferdinand and his wife Sophie lie in state.**

**The Battle of the Marne, September 1914. By halting the German advance, the Allies ensured a long and bitter conflict.**

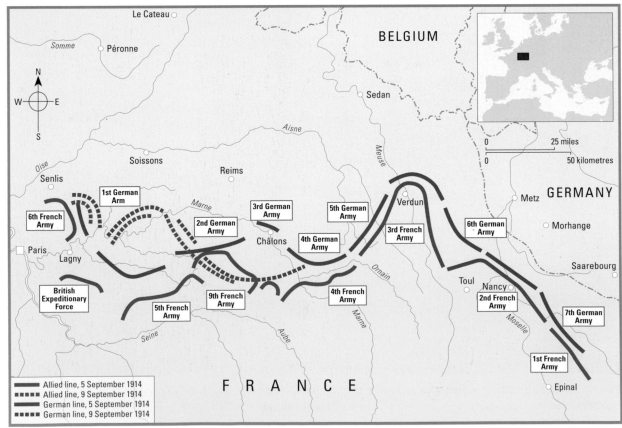

The battle turned out to have been one of the most decisive of modern history. The failure of the Schlieffen Plan forced Germany to fight on two fronts, in the west against Britain and France, and in the east against Russia. In the end this proved more than it could stand. Moreover, the battle virtually ended the war of movement in Western Europe. Unable to out-manoeuvre each other, the two sides swiftly settled to long-drawn-out and costly campaigns of trench warfare (see pages 10-11).

**TRENCH WARFARE** The classic strategy of armies facing one another is to seek to outflank (get round behind) their enemy. This is precisely what the

## TIMETABLE OF THE BATTLE OF THE MARNE

| | |
|---|---|
| 14-25 August | Germans advance on all fronts towards Paris. |
| 31 August | Germans within 50 km of Paris. |
| 4 September | General Kluck moves south-east of Paris, crossing River Marne. This is seen by Allied spotter planes. |
| 6 September | French and British counterattack on Kluck's right flank. |
| 6-8 September | Fierce fighting all along the line. |
| 9 September | Kluck orders his army to withdraw. German commander-in-chief, General von Moltke, orders withdrawal to the River Aisne, north of Paris. |

French soldiers in action during the Battle of the Marne, September 1914. At this early stage of the war soldiers were not equipped with either camouflaged uniforms or steel helmets.

**Temporary shelters that became home – German soldiers in hastily-constructed trenches, 1914.**

## TROUBLE WITH WATER

One of the great problems of trench warfare, as Captain J.I. Cohen wrote from Ypres in 1915, was drainage,

'*This horrible country is made of mud, water and dead Germans. Whenever water is left in a trench it drags the earth down on either side and forms a fearfully sticky viscous matter that lets you sink gently down and grips you like a vice when you're there. … Cover is got by building … dug-outs, behind the trench. Two walls of sandbags with a sheet of corrugated iron on top and an oil-sheet under it to make the whole waterproof.*'

[Quoted in *The Imperial War Museum Book of the First World War*, edited by Malcolm Brown]

Allies (French and British) and the Germans tried to do after the Battle of the Marne. But as one side moved, so the other moved with them. This stretched the front line so that it eventually ran from the Belgian coast to the Swiss border.

Improved military technology – in particular, barbed wire, machine guns and heavy artillery – made a frontal attack almost impossible. To protect themselves, troops on either side dug lines of trenches, usually three deep. These filthy, dangerous holes became the hallmark of the war, both on the Western Front and elsewhere.

World War I was the first to be fought between large industrialized nations. Power depended as much upon industrial output – ships, artillery, rifles, and so forth – as on human muscle. Pinned down by barbed wire, and at the mercy of streams of quick-fire bullets and bombardment by high-explosive shells, the individual soldier became just a statistic: categorized as either able-bodied, wounded, or dead. The war they fought had little to do with glory or valour; it was about 'attrition', grinding the enemy down until they (or you) could take no more.

The trench line from Switzerland to the Channel was complete by the beginning of winter. At the time, it was not seen as in any way permanent. On 30 October, for example, the Germans began a series of attacks on a salient [bulge] in the Allied line around

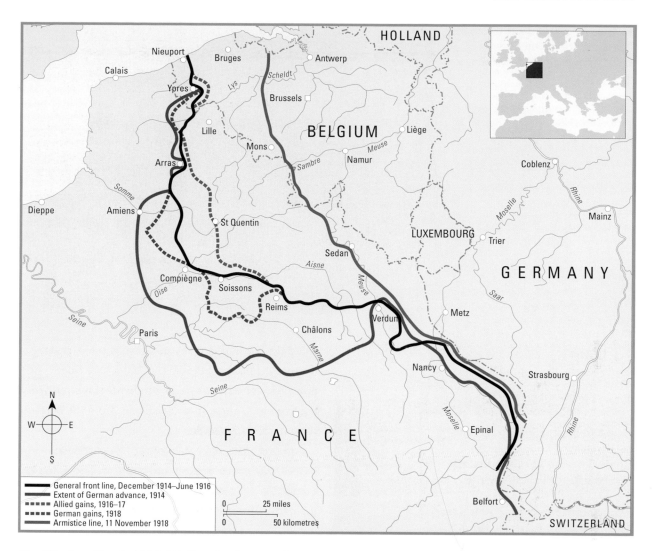

Legend:
- General front line, December 1914–June 1916
- Extent of German advance, 1914
- Allied gains, 1916–17
- German gains, 1918
- Armistice line, 11 November 1918

0    25 miles
0    50 kilometres

**The Western Front, 1914-18. The dominance of defensive technology meant that the line moved little in over four years of fighting.**

the town of Ypres in Belgium. The fighting lasted until 24 November. Although very little ground was gained, the casualties were shocking: 58,200 British, some 50,000 French, and 134,300 Germans. The full horror of mechanized [trench] warfare had begun to be seen.

## THE EASTERN FRONT, 1914-15

The Russian Empire entered the war with enthusiasm. Loyalty to the all-powerful emperor, Nicholas II, swelled and his massive armies assembled quicker than anticipated. By mid-August 1914 two armies, commanded by Generals Pavel Rennenkampf and Alexander Samsonov, were advancing into Prussia, in north-east Germany. However, although moving less

**French soldiers operate a captured German machine gun. Weapons like this took a terrible toll of human life in the war of attrition on the Western Front.**

**Splendid-looking but redundant – as all cavalry, these Russian Cossacks were easy targets for machine gun and artillery fire.**

**The Eastern Front along which the mighty Russian Empire battled against the empires of Germany and Austria-Hungary.**

slowly than expected, they also proved easier to halt.

The Russian commanders did not get on, making communication between their two armies at best patchy. Furthermore, the German commanders, Generals Paul von Hindenburg and Erich Ludendorff, managed to pick up uncoded Russian radio signals. These gave invaluable information about enemy troops numbers and movements.

In late August the Germans split the Russian armies and

## CASUALTIES ON THE EASTERN FRONT, 1914

|  | Killed or wounded | Taken prisoner |
|---|---|---|
| Russian | 617,000 | 182,000 |
| German | 115,000 | – |
| Austro-Hungarian | 400,000 | 100,000 |

These remarkable statistics reveal that in just five months of fighting well over a million soldiers had been lost and over one quarter of a million taken prisoner. The Russians alone had lost almost 800,000 (killed, wounded and captured).

crushed Samsonov's isolated force around the town of Tannnenberg in East Prussia. After the battle (26-30 August) the disgraced Russian commander committed suicide. The Germans then turned on Rennenkampf, outmanoeuvred him, and defeated him at the Battle of Masurian Lakes (9-14 September). By the autumn the Russians were once more back behind their own frontiers.

Further south, in Galicia, the Russians faced the armies of the Austro-Hungarian Empire. Ruled since the thirteenth century by the Habsburg family, the Austro-Hungarian Empire was one of the oldest in Europe. Its territory stretched from Bohemia (modern-day Czech Republic) to Bosnia in the Balkans.

The idea behind this European empire of many peoples and cultures was somewhat out of date. Held together by a vast bureaucracy and loyalty to Emperor Franz Joseph I, it was less well-suited to industrial war than Germany. In Galicia, after initial setbacks, the Russians pushed the multi-national Austro-Hungarian forces back and advanced along a wide front until halted by the rugged terrain of the Carpathian Mountains.

By Christmas 1914, the situation on much of the Eastern Front was similar – thought less rigid – to that in the West. Millions of men, sheltered within frozen trenches, faced each other across barely 100 metres of barren 'no-man's-land'.

**Too young to die? Russian prisoners of war after the decisive Battle of the Masurian Lakes, September 1914, included this very young soldier.**

**THE BALKANS** Given the region's troubled history (the mixture of peoples of different ethnic backgrounds and religious beliefs had led to many conflicts in the past), it is little surprise that the fighting in the Balkans was as ferocious and costly as anywhere. It began in 1914 with a massive Austro-Hungarian attack on Serbia. Fighting to defend their native land, the Serbs proved fierce fighters. Out of a population of some five million, they raised an army of half a million and even drew on the services of women. The invaders were repeatedly driven back with heavy losses.

In 1915 the tide turned. Bulgaria joined the war on the side of the Central Powers and Germany sent 300,000 troops to assist its ally. Utterly overwhelmed, the Serbs fought on to the end of year and some escaped to join Allied forces elsewhere. Nevertheless, by 1916 Serbia was out of the war and Austria-Hungary's power now reached to the frontiers of Greece and Albania.

Romania, wooed by both sides, eventually joined the war on the side of the Allies in August 1916. It proved a costly mistake. Russia was by this time exhausted, leaving the 500,000-strong Romanian army exposed to an attack by a combined force of Austro-Hungarians, Bulgarians, Turks and Germans. By the end of the year Bucharest, the capital city, had fallen. Four hundred thousand men and three-quarters of the country's territory were lost.

Another area of fighting in the Balkans was at Salonika, a port in neutral Greece. Here, in an attempt

> ## KNOWING THE TERRAIN
>
> A British journalist describes how the Serbian commander General Mishitch used his local knowledge to defeat the Austro-Hungarian attack of December 1914:
>
> *'He suddenly advanced in a general attack, on the morning of December 3rd, 1914, and completely surprised the Austro-Hungarians. He caught them leisurely moving along the valley paths. Capturing the overlooking hills, the Serbs shot the hostile columns down, while the Austro-Hungarians were still wondering where they should place their artillery. Naturally, the Serbs knew every rise and fall of the ground, for Mishitch himself had been born and bred [there].'*
>
> [Quoted in *The Great War*, edited by H.W. Wilson and J.A. Hammerton]

**British soldiers in a cheerful mood after landing at Salonika in Greece on their way to reinforce their hard-pressed Serbian allies to the north.**

to assist Serbia in 1915, the Allies landed a force of British and French troops which moved north towards Serbia. It came too late to help the Serbs, however, and was too small to do much on its own. Relatively secure behind their barbed wire, the Allied troops made no notable advance until September 1918. By then the war was almost over. Extraordinarily, the maintenance of the Salonika Front cost almost 500,000 casualties, 18,000 from the war and the rest from disease.

**To the surprise of many, Serbia held out against the numerically superior Austro-Hungarians and fell to the Central Powers only when German troops joined the invasion in 1915.**

**A Serbian howitzer prepares to fire on the invading Austrians, 1915. With no direct link to the sea, Serbia could not easily receive Allied munitions.**

## CHAPTER 2: THE FIGHTING SPREADS

**In vain seeking the Gallipoli break-out: an Allied heavy field gun in action at Helles Bay on the tip of the Gallipoli peninsula, 1915.**

The Turkish Ottoman Empire, a friend of Germany before the war, entered the conflict on the side of the Central Powers in November 1914. This had little immediate impact on the conflict, other than threatening British-held Egypt and forcing Russia to open yet another front to the east of the Black Sea. The following year, however, Turkey was involved in a major campaign that, had it succeeded, might have altered the whole course of the war.

In February and March 1915 British and French warships tried to force their way through the Dardanelles, the narrow neck of water that links the Mediterranean to the Black Sea. The aim, strongly backed by Britain's Winston Churchill, the First Lord of the Admiralty, was to seize Constantinople (modern-day Istanbul) and open a sea route to Russia. Had this been achieved, there was a possibility that the Allies would be able to threaten the Central Powers from the east.

### LANDING AT GALLIPOLI

The naval operation was a failure. Three ships were sunk by Turkish mines and the heavy shore guns remained intact. Undaunted, the Allies turned to a different strategy: a landing on the Gallipoli Peninsula than runs up the western side of the Dardanelles. In April 75,000 British, French and Anzac (Australia and New Zealand Army Corps) men went ashore on different points of the toe of the peninsula. Some met almost no resistance and, had they pressed inland, might have quickly secured a sound base.

The Allied commanders were too hesitant or simply incompetent, and the important advantage was lost. The Turkish resistance, well organized by the German General Liman von Sanders, kept the Allies pinned down on

**The Gallipoli Campaign, 1915-16. Although daring and original in concept, the Allied plan failed through gross mismanagement on the ground and because of the courage of the Turkish resistance.**

### Map

Royal Naval Division

Turkish 7th Division

AEGEAN SEA

Gallipoli

GALLIPOLI PENINSULA

Suvla Bay

Second British landings

Anzac Cove

ANZAC

Dardanelles

Maidos

Turkish 9th Division

Chanak Kale

TURKEY

Krithia

First British landings

Cape Helles

French

Kum Kale

0  5 miles
0  5 kilometres

N
W E
S

← Allied landings
←- Allied feint attacks
/// Area captured by Allies
● Turkish fort
⬤ Turkish batteries
⁙ Turkish minefield

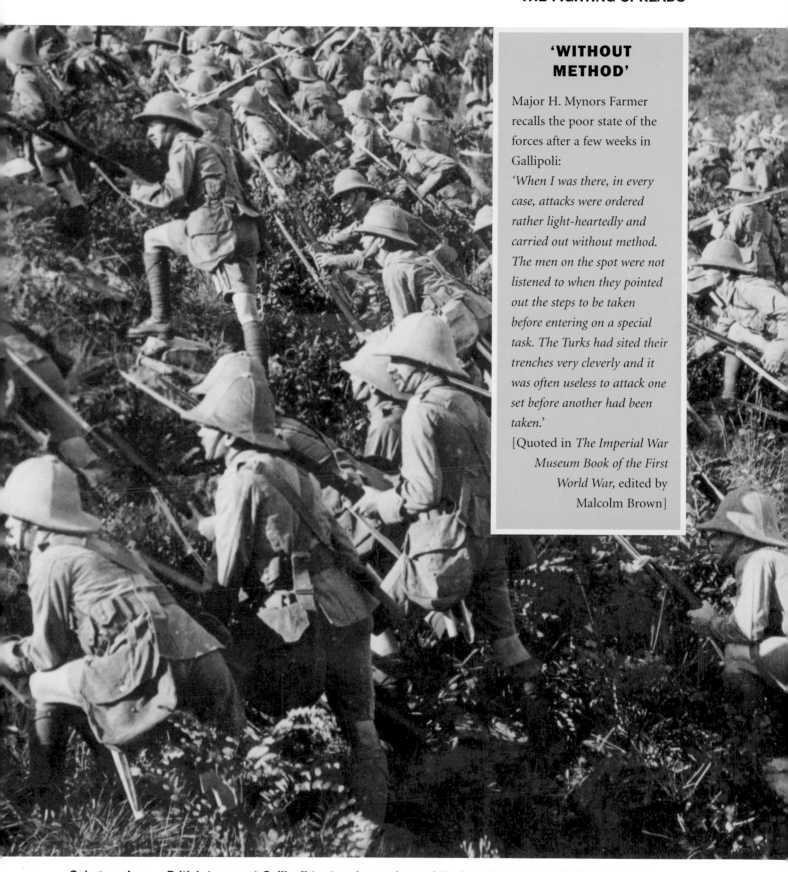

Major H. Mynors Farmer recalls the poor state of the forces after a few weeks in Gallipoli:

*'When I was there, in every case, attacks were ordered rather light-heartedly and carried out without method. The men on the spot were not listened to when they pointed out the steps to be taken before entering on a special task. The Turks had sited their trenches very cleverly and it was often useless to attack one set before another had been taken.'*

[Quoted in *The Imperial War Museum Book of the First World War*, edited by Malcolm Brown]

Going nowhere – British troops at Gallipoli try to advance beyond the beaches, August 1915. Time and again they were thrown back by the well-organized Turkish defences.

the beaches. A second landing in August was equally ineffective.

In October the decision was taken to withdraw, an operation completed by January 1916. So ended one of the major fiascos of the war, a dismal catalogue of poor planning and incompetent leadership that produced some 250,000 casualties on either side.

## NORTHERN ITALY

Italy's agreements with Germany and Austria-Hungary did not oblige it to enter the war on their side in 1914. This was just as well because at the time its armed forces were in poor shape – there were only 600 machine guns in the entire country, for example. Nevertheless, the temptation to join the war proved too great to resist, and the following year (May 1915) it sided with the Allies in the hope of gaining territory from Austria-Hungary.

The war did not go well for the Italians. They remained short of weapons and munitions, both of which were supplied in large quantities by Britain and France. Furthermore, as is clear from a glance at the map, the Austro-Hungarians held the key strategic positions in the mountains overlooking the Italian lines.

**Fighting the enemy – and the weather. Troops of the Italian Alpine Regiment prepare for action in the snowy Alps, 1915.**

The American novelist Ernest Hemingway served as a volunteer with an ambulance unit on the Italian Front. He based his novel *A Farewell To Arms* (1929) directly on his experiences. This is how he describes the scene in the first chapter of the book:

'*There were mists over the river and clouds on the mountain and the trucks splashed mud on the road and the troops were muddy and wet in their capes; their rifles were wet …*

*At the start of the winter came permanent rain and with the rain came cholera. But it was checked and in the end only seven thousand died of it in the army.*'

[From *A Farewell To Arms*, Ernest Hemingway]

withdrawal halted only on the River Piave, 110 km from the Isonzo. Around 275,000 Italians had been captured. On the Piave the Italians managed to dig in and rebuild. Assisted by Allied reinforcements, the new commander, General Armando Diaz, launched a final offensive in October 1918 against an enemy that was by now dispirited and exhausted from sustaining years of fighting on two fronts. The Allies advanced swiftly along a broad

**Austrian troops armed with flame-throwers advance along the Isonzo River, 1916.**

**The front in north-east Italy. The easy gains that Italy hoped for when it joined the war in 1915 were not forthcoming.**

Austria-Hungary found it hard enough managing its long front with Russia, so to begin with it was content to resist Italian assaults. Between 1915-17 the Italians launched eleven full-scale offensives in the region, none of which managed to seize more than a few kilometres of ground. After the last, made in the late summer of 1917, the Italian commander General Luigi Cadorna decided to build up his defences to face an expected attack by German as well as Austro-Hungarian forces.

The Central Powers' attack of 24 October-12 November 1917, known as the Battle of Caporetto, was a total disaster for the Italian Army. German forces advanced 23 km on the first day, and the Italian

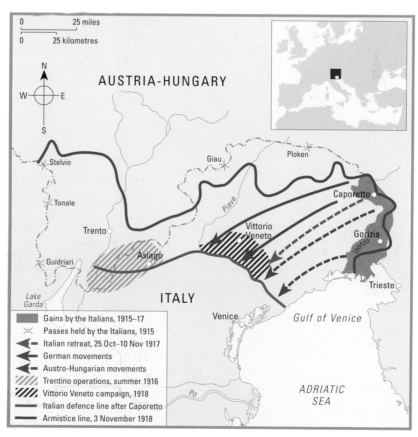

Hail the victor! The British General Allenby rides into Jerusalem after driving the Turks from the city, December 1917.

front until Austria-Hungary signed an armistice on 3 November 1918, bringing hostilities between that country and the Allies to a close (see also page 50).

**MIDDLE EAST** The war extended into the Middle East when the fleet of the Turkish Ottoman Empire bombarded Russian Black Sea ports without warning on 29 October 1914. Declarations of war soon followed. In alliance with the Central Powers, who provided officers and munitions for the depleted Turkish Army, Turkey fought on four fronts. On only one, Gallipoli (see pages 14-15), did it achieve success.

In the north the Turks launched an attack on southern Russia (the Caucasus) in an attempt to seize the region's oilfields. At the Battle of Sarikamish (29 December 1914 to 3 January 1915) they were roundly defeated, suffering 30,000 casualties and losing much of the remainder of their army as prisoners of war.

## TROUBLE AHEAD

Eager for support, British politicians made conflicting offers to their allies. They promised the Arabs independence, and the Jews a national homeland in Palestine. Foreign Minister Lord Balfour's letter to Lord Rothschild, the leader of Britain's Jews, proved to be one of the seeds of the modern Arab-Israeli conflict.

*'His Majesty's Government view with favour the establishment in Palestine of a national home for the Jewish people, and will use their best endeavours to facilitate the achievement of this object, it being clearly understood that nothing shall be done which may prejudice the civil and religious rights of existing non-Jewish communities in Palestine, or the rights and political status enjoyed by Jews in any other country.'*
2 November 1917.

[Quoted in *Arab-Israeli Conflict and Conciliation: A Documentary History*, edited by Bernard Reich]

In the eastern corner of their empire, in the region of Mesopotamia (modern-day Iraq) at the head of the Persian Gulf, the Turks faced an invasion by an Anglo-Indian army sent from British-held India. At first the invaders made swift progress, taking the region's oilfields. The Turks regained the initiative in 1916 when they took 8,000 Anglo-Indian prisoners at Kut al Imara. By the time hostilities ended, however, the British had again moved forward, capturing Baghdad (March 1917) and advancing further up the Tigris and Euphrates rivers.

The Suez canal in Egypt, a key route between Britain and India, the jewel in its imperial crown, was an obvious target for the Turks. Knowing this, the British built up strong defences, resisted Turkish assaults in 1914-15, and pressed on into Sinai in 1916-17. They were assisted by a widespread revolt among the Arab peoples, eager to be rid of their Turkish overlords.

Held up for a while at Gaza, at the end of 1917 the Allies seized Jerusalem in Palestine. The large Anglo-Arab force, commanded by the able General Sir

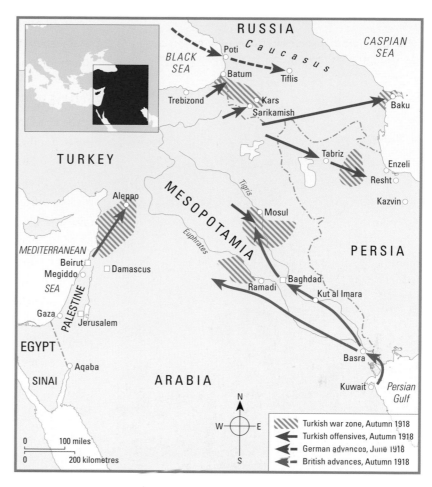

Fighting in the Near and Middle East, where the Turkish Ottoman Empire fought the Russians and the British, and also struggled to hold down a revolt of the Arabs.

**Battling for the Empire –
Indian gunners defend
the British-held Suez
Canal against a Turkish
attack.**

**21**

Edmund Allenby, then destroyed the remaining Turkish forces in the region at the Battle of Megiddo, and moved forward to occupy Damascus in Syria on 1 October 1918.

**AFRICA** The Middle East was not the limit of the fighting. The conflict became truly global as early as 1914, when Japan, an ally of Britain, seized German colonies in the Pacific Ocean and in mainland China. There was fighting in Africa, too. Here Allied

## LOSSES IN AFRICA

**Cameroons**

| | |
|---|---|
| Britain | 2,300 killed, wounded and captured |
| France | 3,900 killed, wounded and captured |
| Germany | 6,575 killed, wounded and captured |

**South-West Africa**

| | |
|---|---|
| South Africa | 1,760 killed, wounded and captured |
| Germany | 4,580 killed, wounded and captured |

**East Africa**

| | |
|---|---|
| Allies | 51,600 killed or died of disease |
| | 8,800 wounded |
| | 1,900 captured |
| Germany* | 5,000 killed and wounded |
| | 6,000 captured |

\* Figures no more than estimates

**War East African style! A British soldier seated on an ox during the long campaign to hunt down the brilliant German General Paul von Lettow-Vorbeck.**

1914. The same two countries gradually occupied the Cameroons, 1914-17. On the outbreak of war South Africa offered to undertake the capture of German South-West Africa. This was achieved by four columns, totalling 50,000 men, over a period of ten months.

In contrast, German resistance in East Africa continued throughout the war. This was largely due to the leadership of General Paul von Lettow-Vorbeck, a brilliant guerrilla commander. In 1914 he had a mere 2,750 men (of whom 2,500 were Africans) to hold a territory the size of France. Later this rose to 14,000 (11,000 Africans). Against him were ranged almost the entire South African Army and many European and local troops and assistants, totalling at their peak 350,000 men. This was precisely what Lettow-Vorbeck wanted – to divert as many

forces from Britain, France and their colonies assaulted the four German colonies in Africa: Togoland (Togo), the Cameroons (Cameroon), German South-West Africa (Namibia), and German East Africa (Tanzania). The aim was to seize territory and shut down the powerful German radio stations that were monitoring Allied shipping.

Togo fell swiftly to French and British troops in

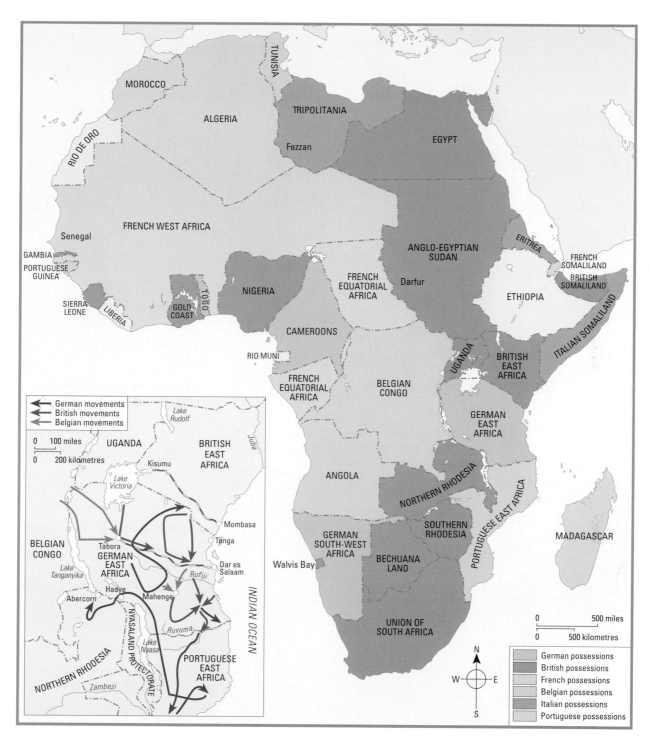

**Africa during World War I. The continent was drawn into the fighting because during the previous century it had been carved up by the imperial European powers. The inset shows the campaign in German East Africa.**

Allied soldiers as possible from the battles in Europe (see statistics panel).

After a successful but costly attack early in 1915, Lettow-Vorbeck decided to stick to hit-and-run guerrilla tactics. He used local conditions and speed of movement to great effect. A successful tactic was to build up a strong defensive position, hold it for a while in order to inflict maximum casualties on the attackers, then slip away before the final assault. Only when he heard of the Armistice (see page 49) did the

## COMPARATIVE NAVAL STRENGTHS, 1914

| Allies | Britain | France | Russia | Italy | Japan | USA* | Totals |
|---|---|---|---|---|---|---|---|
| New-style battleships (dreadnoughts) | 22 | 8 | 0 | 3 | 2 | 10 | 45 |
| Old-style battleships | 40 | 14 | 10 | 7 | 10 | 23 | 104 |
| Cruisers | 130 | 28 | 12 | 21 | 34 | 34 | 259 |
| Destroyers | 221 | 81 | 25 | 33 | 50 | 50 | 460 |
| Torpedo boats | 109 | 187 | 72 | 80 | 0 | 23 | 471 |
| Submarines | 73 | 70 | 22 | 23 | 12 | 18 | 218 |

\* By the time the United States entered the war in 1917, all fleets were larger.

| Central Powers | Germany | A-Hungary | Turkey | Totals |
|---|---|---|---|---|
| New-style battleships (dreadnoughts) | 15 | 6 | 0 | 21 |
| Old-style battleships | 22 | 6 | 2 | 30 |
| Cruisers | 57 | 7 | 2 | 66 |
| Destroyers | 90 | 18 | 8 | 116 |
| Torpedo boats | 115 | 65 | 9 | 189 |
| Submarines | 31 | 5 | 0 | 36 |

The foredeck and main guns of the German battleship *Braunschweig* pictured at the start of the war in 1914.

undefeated Lettow-Vorbeck finally surrender on 23 November 1918.

**WAR AT SEA** Naval warfare had been revolutionized during the fifty years before 1914. Huge steel battleships, driven by steam turbines and armed with massive shell-firing guns in turrets, had made all other large warships obsolete. However, these remarkable vessels were vulnerable to mines (as we saw in the Dardanelles, pages 16-17) and torpedoes. The latter could now be delivered with great accuracy by submarines. Finally, the use of spotter aircraft and radio enabled commanders to know their enemy's precise location and movements.

Essentially, the naval war developed into one of blockades – the Allies seeking to cut Germany and Austria-Hungary's overseas supplies of food and raw materials, while the Germans tried to do the same to Britain and France. In the end, it was the Allied blockade that succeeded, bringing Germany to its knees in the autumn of 1918.

Germany' chief hope of breaking the Allied blockade lay in sailing its High Seas Fleet past the British Grand Fleet into the open oceans. After some

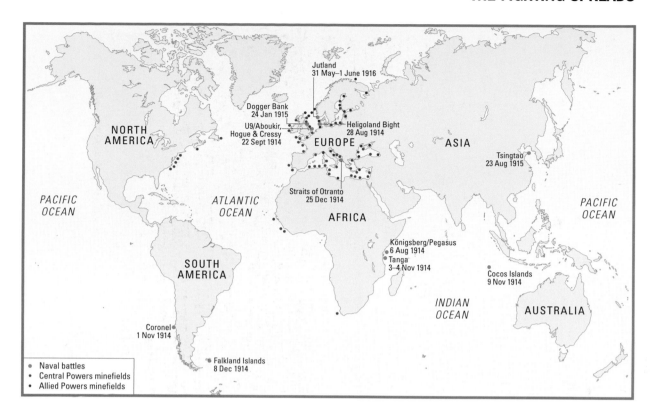

Jutland
31 May–1 June 1916

Dogger Bank
24 Jan 1915

U9/Aboukir,
Hogue & Cressy
22 Sept 1914

Heligoland Bight
28 Aug 1914

NORTH
AMERICA

EUROPE

ASIA

Tsingtao
23 Aug 1915

PACIFIC
OCEAN

ATLANTIC
OCEAN

Straits of Otranto
25 Dec 1914

AFRICA

PACIFIC
OCEAN

SOUTH
AMERICA

Königsberg/Pegasus
6 Aug 1914

Tanga
3–4 Nov 1914

Cocos Islands
9 Nov 1914

INDIAN
OCEAN

AUSTRALIA

Coronel
1 Nov 1914

Falkland Islands
8 Dec 1914

• Naval battles
• Central Powers minefields
• Allied Powers minefields

early naval encounters at Coronel, the Falkland Islands (both 1914), and in the North Sea (1914-15), in May 1916 Admiral Reinhard Scheer decided to attempt this full-scale break-out. The German High Seas Fleet met the British Grand Fleet at the Battle of Jutland, the only major naval engagement of World War I. The British suffered greater losses but drove the Germans back to port, where they remained for the rest of the war. After Jutland the Germans relied on submarines, known as U-boats, to sever Allied supply lines. For an effective blockade, U-boats needed to attack all shipping – neutral or Allied – destined for Britain and France. This tactic infuriated the US and helped bring it into the war on the Allied side in April 1917. By 1918 the use of convoys and improved anti-submarine weapons (for example, the depth charge, 1916) had finally broken the U-boat's dangerous stranglehold.

**WAR IN THE AIR** The wartime development of aircraft technology was dramatic, driven mainly by the need to conduct aerial observation of enemy artillery, and to prevent the enemy from doing this themselves. In 1914 warplanes were slow, fairly unreliable, incapable of carrying heavy loads, and used

**The naval war. Apart from the major engagement between the British and German fleets at Jutland, 1916, conflicts were small scale, involving no more than a handful of vessels on either side.**

**A Fairey F.17 seaplane, 1917. The emergence of such aircraft enabled fleet commanders to keep track of the enemy with much greater accuracy.**

**A German naval Zeppelin airship taking off from its base. Although capable of flying huge distances, Zeppelins were slow and vulnerable to enemy fire.**

**Early bombing – a British aircrew prepares to drop its aircraft's lightweight bombs by hand. Inevitably, the accuracy of the bombing was rather hit and miss.**

largely for reconnaissance work. By 1918 they had become much more powerful and reliable, and were designed with specific tasks in mind. They were also organized as a separate branch of the armed forces, such as the Royal Air Force (1918), and were seen as a vital element in any military or naval operation. Air superiority, which the Allies had achieved by 1918, was key to success on the ground. The major Allied offensive of September 1918, for example, took place under cover provided by over 450 aircraft.

One of the first specialist aircraft to appear was the fast and manoeuvrable fighter, designed to shoot down enemy aircraft in 'dogfights'. A popular example was the British Sopwith Camel. The French Breugets were

among the earliest bombers. The Italian SIA 7 was intended specifically for reconnaissance, the German Halberstadt CL11 for attacking troops on the ground, and the Short 184 for carrying torpedoes.

A German speciality was the gas-filled airship, known as the Zeppelin, used for long-range bombing. Able to rise to 6,700 m (higher than any aircraft before 1916) and carry 1,000 kg of bombs, they killed 550 civilians in raids on Britain. Once aircraft could reach the same height as a Zeppelin, however, the cumbersome 'sausages' (as they were known) became easy targets.

In 1918 two aircraft appeared that signposted the future. One was Germany's sleek and rapid Junkers D1,

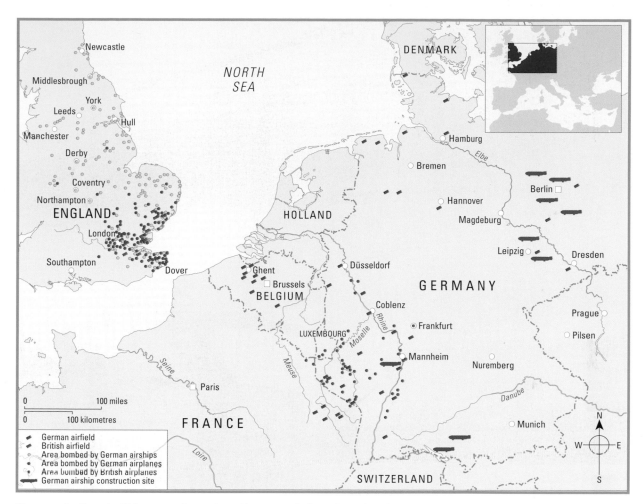

**The war in the air. This map shows how the use of aircraft as bombers meant that no one on the ground, neither soldier nor civilian, was safe from attack.**

the world's first all-metal warplane. The other was Britain's Handley Page V/1500, a four-engined bomber capable of carrying 2,000 kg of bombs and staying airborne for fourteen hours. With aircraft such these, no one, neither soldier nor civilian, was safe. Thus World War I saw the emergence of the 'home front' – war waged against the civil population of a country – alongside the traditional battle front.

## THE GROWTH OF AIR FORCES

| Number of aircraft | France | Britain* | Italy | USA | Russia | Germany | A-Hungary |
|---|---|---|---|---|---|---|---|
| 1914 | 150 | 50 | 120 | | 145 | 250 | 80 |
| 1915 | 390 | 153 | 240 | | 553 | 800 | 112 |
| 1916 | 1,420 | 410 | 430 | | 724 | 1,550 | 144 |
| 1917 | 2,335 | 997 | 660 | 55 | 579 | 2,270 | 296 |
| 1918 | 3,222 | 1,799 | 720 | 740 | 260 | 2,710 | 616 |

* Western Front only

Note that not all of these aircraft were of military use. Of the 55 aircraft available to the United States in April 1917, for instance, 51 were obsolete.

# CHAPTER 3: DEADLOCK, 1915-17

During 1915, particularly after the failure of the Allied Gallipoli expedition (see pages 16-17), it was generally recognized that the fighting on the Western Front was now critical and that the war would be won or lost there. Here, at the direct interface between Germany, France and Britain where the front lines confronted one another, the fighting became more and more costly.

At the start of the year commanders on both sides, especially the Allied one, hoped that a quick breakthrough would end the stalemate on the Western Front and bring the war to a rapid conclusion. However, as they found time and time again, while seizing three lines of enemy trenches was difficult enough, co-ordinating an advance after that proved just about impossible. In March 1915, for instance, the British broke through at Neuve-Chapelle in northern France but, after advancing 2 km, the attack ground to a halt. The story was similar the next month, when the Germans, using poison gas for the first time, broke through at Ypres in Belgium. When the battle stopped

One of the millions of victims – a French soldier killed in the 1915 campaign in the Champagne region.

Walking through hell: German reinforcements move up to the front line during the Champagne offensive of 1915.

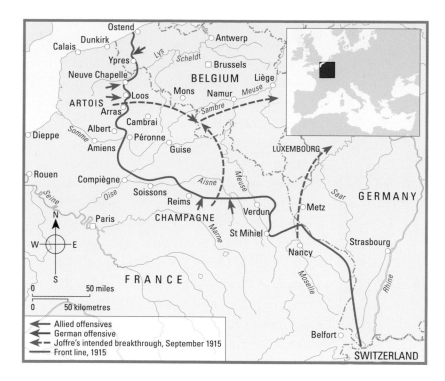

**The breakthrough that never came: the Allied plan for the spring offensive of 1915 that it was hoped would win the war at a stroke.**

## IN THE FRONT LINES

Although it is a novel, *All Quiet on the Western Front* by the German soldier Erich Remarque is widely recognized as one of the finest accounts of life on the Western Front. This is his description of bombardment:

*'An uncertain red glow spreads along the skyline from one end to the other. It is in perpetual movement, punctuated with bursts of flame from the nozzles of the batteries … French rockets go up, which unfold a silk parachute to the air and drift slowly down. They light up everything as bright as day … "Bombardment," says Kat. The thunder of the guns swells to a single heavy roar and then breaks up again into separate explosions. The dry bursts of the machine guns rattle. Above us, the air teems with invisible swift movement, with howls, pipings, and hisses …'*

[From *All Quiet On the Western Front*, Erich Remarque]

on 25 May they had done no more than flatten out the Ypres salient. German and Allied casualties totalled 103,000.

In May the British and French went on the offensive again, this time in the Artois region. As before, in some places the attackers managed to break through the enemy lines but they made little progress after that. September saw the launching of a massive offensive that was to smash through the German lines in Champagne and allow the French to sweep north into Belgium. After a 2,500-gun bombardment, 500,000 French troops attacked along a 24-km front. The same pattern emerged: some initial gains, then stagnation, and horrific casualty rates. By 28 September the French had lost 145,000 men.

As the Champagne offensive was grinding to a halt, an Anglo-French offensive started further north in the Artois region of France. The French lost 48,000 men for negligible gains, while the incompetent leadership of Sir John French, commander of the British army in France, bungled the promising British breakthrough around the village of Loos (25 September to 4 November).

**THE BATTLE AT VERDUN** Unknown to each other, both sides planned even bigger offensives for 1916. They hoped for breakthrough, of course, but there was a growing recognition that this might not be possible. In its place came the concept of attrition (see pages 10-11) – a war that would be won only when the enemy were either too depleted or too exhausted to fight on.

While the Allies planned a summer offensive near the River Somme,

at the junction of the French and British armies, the German commander General Erich von Falkenhayn hoped to break France's spirit by continual assault on a narrow front that was difficult to defend. His target was Verdun, a city that for historical reasons he knew the French would defend

**Counterattack! French troops defending their line in the Verdun region go over the top in a counteroffensive against the encircling Germans in 1916.**

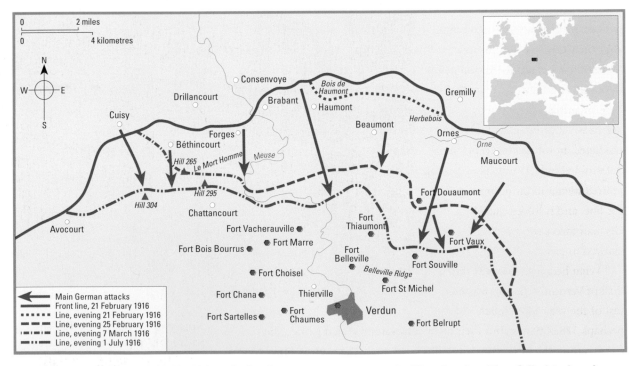

0 ——— 2 miles
0 ——— 4 kilometres

N
W ✥ E
S

Consenvoye
Bois de Haumont
Gremilly
Drillancourt
Brabant
Haumont
Cuisy
Forges
Beaumont
Herbebois
Béthincourt
Ornes
Hill 265
Le Mort Homme
Meuse
Orne
Maucourt
Hill 304
Hill 295
Avocourt
Chattancourt
Fort Douaumont
Fort Vacherauville ●
Fort Thiaumont
Fort Marre ●
Fort Vaux ●
Fort Bois Bourrus ●
Fort Belleville ●
Fort Souville
Fort Choisel ●
Belleville Ridge
Fort St Michel ●
Fort Chana ●
Thierville
Fort Sartelles ●
Fort Chaumes ●
Verdun
Fort Belrupt ●

← Main German attacks
—— Front line, 21 February 1916
····· Line, evening 21 February 1916
▬▬▬ Line, evening 25 February 1916
▬·▬· Line, evening 7 March 1916
▬··▬·· Line, evening 1 July 1916

**The Verdun campaign of 1916. Although the Germans made some significant gains, they failed to break through or crush the spirit of the French Army.**

## VERDUN IN PERSPECTIVE

French and German losses in just one battle in 1916 exceeded those of all major combatant nations during fighting in the previous year.

**Losses in 1915**

|  | French | British | German | Total |
|---|---|---|---|---|
| Neuve-Chapelle - |  | 13,000 | 7,000 | 20,000 |
| Ypres | 10,000 | 59,000 | 35,000 | 104,000 |
| Artois | 102,000 | 28,000 | 49,000 | 179,000 |
| Champagne | 143,000 |  | 85,000 | 228,000 |
| Artois-Loos | 48,000 | 61,000 | 56,000 | 165,000 |
|  | **303,000** | **161,000** | **232,000** | **696,000** |

**Losses in the Battle of Verdun, 1916**

| French | 378,000 |
|---|---|
| German | 337,000 |
|  | **715,000** |

to the last man. Here, he undertook to 'bleed' the French army to death. The German attack on Verdun began on 21 February 1916. One million men launched themselves on a network of forts that had been left undermanned and under-gunned. Within seventy-two hours, after the Germans had pushed forward more than five kilometres, it looked as if they might well take Verdun and its surrounding defences. As Falkenhayn had predicted, however, the French were determined to hold out. They poured men and munitions into the line, and resolved that the German forces should not be allowed to pass.

What became known as the 'hell of Verdun' raged on for the rest of the year. The French lost perhaps 378,000 men, but their army was not quite bled white. The Germans, on the other hand, lost almost as many themselves. Since they were also fighting on the Eastern Front, where they had to support Austria-Hungary, as well as supplying troops to other theatres

**Happy to be out of it – German prisoners taken at Verdun are paraded through the streets under mounted guard on their way to captivity.**

## OVER THE TOP

British private soldier Roy Bealing remembers going over the top of his trench during an attack on the Somme:

*'When the whistle went, I threw my rifle on top of the trench and clambered out of it, grabbed the rifle and started going forward. There were shell-holes everywhere. I hadn't gone far before I fell in one. … I must have fallen half a dozen times before I got to the first line, and there were lads falling all over the place. You didn't know whether they were just tripping up, like me, or whether they were going down with bullets in them, because it wasn't just the shells exploding round about, it was the machine guns hammering out like hell from the third German line because it was on slightly higher ground.'*

[Quoted in *Somme*, Lyn Macdonald]

of war, such as Africa and the Middle East, the losses were harder for them to bear. Moreover, in July their assault on Verdun had drawn a massive British counter-assault on the Somme.

**THE SOMME** As we saw on page 29, in late 1915 the Allies had planned a joint attack on the Somme for the late summer of 1916. This plan was altered when the Verdun offensive pinned down the bulk of the French Army. In response, the main weight of the Allied attack, which at the request of the French was brought forward by several weeks, would now be borne by the British.

Fix bayonets! British troops prepare to go over the top on the first day of the Battle of the Somme, 1 July 1916. For many this was their first experience of battle; for most of the 60,000 killed and wounded it was also their last.

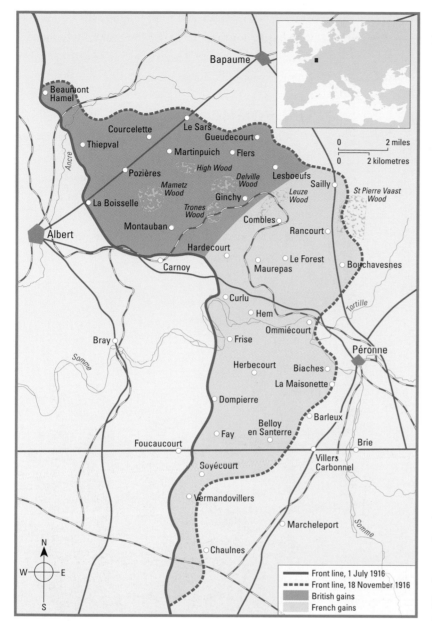

**Field Marshal Sir Douglas Haig (1861-1928), friend of King George V and commander-in-chief of the British forces in France 1915-18.**

**The Battle of the Somme, 1916. The choice of battleground was made not for strategic reasons but because it was where the French and British lines met.**

Before 1914 the British had concentrated their military spending on the Royal Navy. Their regular army ready for European action had consisted only of the 150,000-strong British Expeditionary Force. By 1916 this had been all but wiped out, meaning that the hugely expanded army – now over two million men – was largely made up of eager but inexperienced volunteers. They were joined by the small but highly efficient contingents provided by Canada, South Africa, New Zealand and Australia. It was with these forces, domestic and colonial, that the new British commander, Sir Douglas Haig, hoped to break through the well-arranged German defences on the Somme.

Despite careful preparation and a gigantic eight-day preliminary bombardment of the enemy lines, the first day of the offensive – 1 July 1916 – was the worst ever experienced by a British army. Walking across no-man's-land into intact barbed wire and the deadly fire of machine guns, most of which had survived the artillery bombardment in deep concrete shelters, the attackers were mown down like grass. Some 58,000 men were lost for negligible gains. Only on the southern flank and in the neighbouring French sector was much headway made.

The battle raged on until November, by when the Allies had advanced no more than 16 km at a cost of 613,000 men killed and wounded (419,000 British). Even so, the German Army had suffered equally heavily and, combined with the effects of Verdun and the Brusilov Offensive (see below), by the end of the year was no longer in a fit state to launch an offensive.

## RUSSIA'S LAST CAST

As the British were attempting to take pressure off the French by attacking on the Somme, so the Russians had gathered themselves for one final offensive on the Eastern Front. It was also planned to help their Italian allies by drawing Austro-Hungarian divisions away from the Alps. The general responsible for planning and launching the attack was Alexei Brusilov, probably the most able Russian commander of the war.

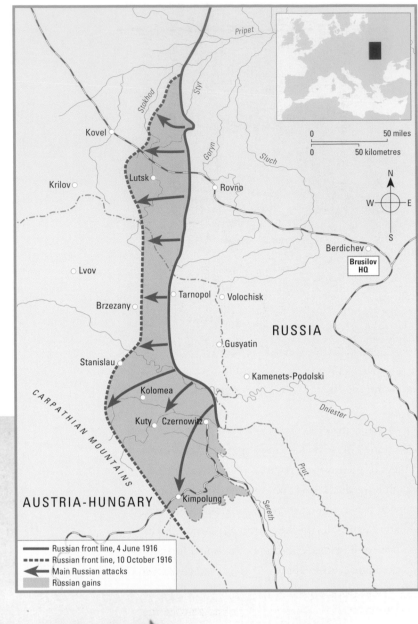

Russian front line, 4 June 1916
Russian front line, 10 October 1916
Main Russian attacks
Russian gains

**Russia's Brusilov Offensive in 1916 forced the Germans to switch troops from the Western Front but brought the Russian army to its knees.**

**Enough is enough – tired of official incompetence and senseless slaughter, Russian soldiers surrender in 1917.**

**The last tsar of Russia, Nicholas II, sits alone after being forced to abdicate his throne in 1917.**

What is now called the 'Brusilov Offensive' began on 4 June 1916. The Russians moved forward in the valleys of the Rivers Prut and Dniester, and further north towards the town of Lutsk. Brusilov placed himself between the two points of attack. His enemy, mostly Austro-Hungarian, were taken somewhat by surprise and fell back in disarray. Within a fortnight the Russians had advanced 80 km and taken almost 100,000 prisoners.

Realizing the danger, both German and Austro-Hungarian reinforcements were rushed to the front, and the Russian advance halted for a while. Twice that summer it was resumed. It met with considerable success against the Austro-Hungarians in the south, where the Russians reached the Carpathian Mountains, but less against the Germans in the north. Finally, in mid-September, Brusilov called off the entire operation. His army had fought itself to a standstill, having lost perhaps 1.4 million men as casualties and prisoners. The figure for his opponents was only slightly less.

Brusilov had been let down by his support services, not by his troops. Sometimes attacks were

## THE MAKE-UP OF THE RUSSIAN ARMY

The Brusilov Offensive was launched with the Russian 3rd, 7th, 8th, 9th and 11th armies. Their strengths and varied make-up were as follows:

**3rd Army**
6 infantry divisions
6 cavalry divisions (5 of Cossacks)
1 reserve division

**7th Army**
9 infantry divisions
2 divisions of Finnish troops
2 cavalry divisions (1 of Cossacks)
3 reserve divisions, including 1 of Turks

**8th Army**
10 infantry divisions
2 divisions of Turkish troops
3 cavalry divisions (1 of Cossacks)
1 division of Finnish troops
2 reserve divisions

**9th Army**
9 infantry divisions
5 cavalry divisions (4 of Cossacks)
1 reserve division

**11th Army**
8 infantry divisions
4 cavalry divisions
1 division of Finnish troops
3 reserve divisions
Total initial strength of all armies: 57 infantry divisions (570,000 men approx.) and 20 cavalry divisions (200,000 men approx.)
(Note: These figures do not include reinforcements who were brought up later.)

halted because the ammunition ran out. On other occasions reinforcements came too late because of the inefficiency of the Russian railway system. Supplies of food and new weapons were at best unreliable, sometimes non-existent. To cap it all, the country's military leadership, from Supreme Commander Tsar

Nicholas II downwards, failed to co-operate or co-ordinate their activities. In short, after the Brusilov Offensive the entire Russian military machine was beginning to fall apart.

### FRANCE GRINDS TO A HALT The most interesting development on the Western Front during 1917 was the German withdrawal to the Hindenburg Line (*Siegfried Stellung*) that ran south in France from Arras to near Soissons. This was a pre-prepared defensive arrangement of barbed wire entanglements, trenches, machine-gun posts and concrete bunkers that proved exceptionally difficult to penetrate by conventional means. Having given up any idea of launching an offensive in this part of the front, the

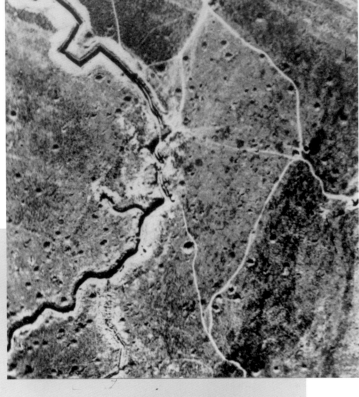

Germany's Hindenburg Line, 1916, peppered with many shell craters.

An army falls apart – French deserters run towards the German lines, Spring 1917. News of events such as this mutiny by serving soldiers was not revealed to the general public.

Germans retired to it between 23 February and 5 April. In contrast, the Allies still hoped for the elusive breakthrough. The new French commander, General Robert Nivelle, well-known for his offensive strategies, believed he could break through the German lines in the region of the River Aisne. His subordinates,

including Marshal Philippe Pétain, strongly advised him to reconsider. He refused.

By way of a diversion, in April the British under Haig attacked near Arras. After the usual bombardment, they made the biggest single-day advance of the war by British forces thus far – five and

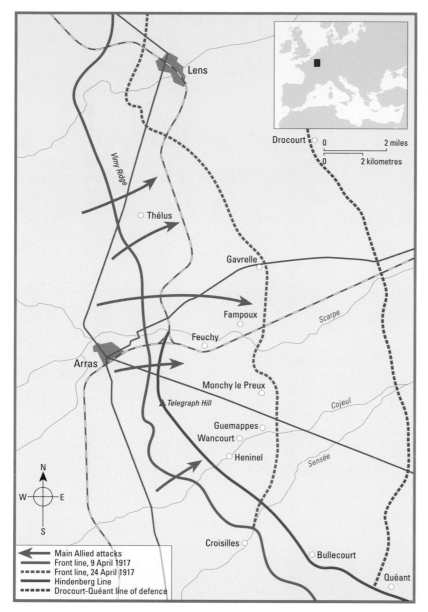

### GASSED

Harold Clegg recalls the effects of a German attack in July 1917 using a new form of gas – mustard gas – that burned away at the organs with which it came into contact.

'Our eyes now began to feel irritated. The tea was instrumental in making all and sundry commence to vomit. After being violently sick I received instructions to prepare myself to join a [guard] party ... I began to scrape the ... mud from my [equipment] ...

'While doing so I heard several men complain about pain in their eyes, some even complaining of going blind.' July 1917.

[Quoted in *The Imperial War Museum Book of the First World War*, edited by Malcolm Brown]

**The Battle of Arras, 1917. The seizure of Vimy Ridge by Canadian forces was one of the most gallant actions of the entire war.**

a half kilometres! Although the fighting continued to mid-May, further gains were very limited before the offensive was called off.

Meanwhile, the French had launched their offensive between Soissons and Reims (positions shown on map on page 29). Yet again, despite the use of tanks (first seen on the Somme), a decisive breakthrough that could release the cavalry over open ground was not achieved. After some early gains, including the capture of 20,000 German soldiers and a section of the Hindenburg Line, the advance floundered to a halt. The casualty rate had been as high as ever – in less than a month Nivelle lost 187,000 of the 1.2 million men under his command. The Germans figure was about 163,000.

The morale of many French troops now broke: a large number simply refused to take part in any further attacks. For a while (April to June 1917) the mutiny threatened to force France out of the war, making a German victory highly probable. Nivelle was promptly sacked and, with great skill, Pétain began the difficult task of pulling his shattered forces together again.

The war of attrition goes on ... and on. Heavily laden British troops moving up to the front line, October 1917.

## THE GERMAN LINE HOLDS

1917 was the crucial year of the war. Russia was in turmoil (see pages 40-1). Austria-Hungary crushed the Italians (see pages 18-19), who were more and more disillusioned with the war. The bulk of the French were in no fit state to do more than hold their line. The German command sensed that victory in the east was near, and a sustained attack on the demoralized French line might, at last, achieve breakthrough. Field Marshal Douglas Haig, the British commander-in-chief, still believed he could pierce the German line with a massive frontal assault.

On top of this came the dramatic development of 6 April 1917 – the United States of America joined the war on the Allied side. Two factors in particular persuaded Congress to take this momentous step. First, early in the year Germany reintroduced unrestricted submarine warfare, which threatened the shipping of the neutral United States. Second, the British intercepted a German telegram offering part of the southern US to Mexico if it would side with the Central Powers. When

### THE ONLY ONE

Private R. Le Brun, a Canadian machine gunner, remembers fighting in the deep November mud around the village of Passchendaele.

*'There was nothing between us and the Germans across the swamp. Three times during the night they shelled us heavily, and we had to keep on spraying bullets into the darkness to keep them from advancing. The night was alive with bullets. By morning, of our team of six, only my buddy Tombes and I were left. Then came the burst that got Tombes. It got him right in the head. ... It was a terrible feeling being the only one left.'*

[Quoted in *They Called it Passchendaele*, Lyn Macdonald]

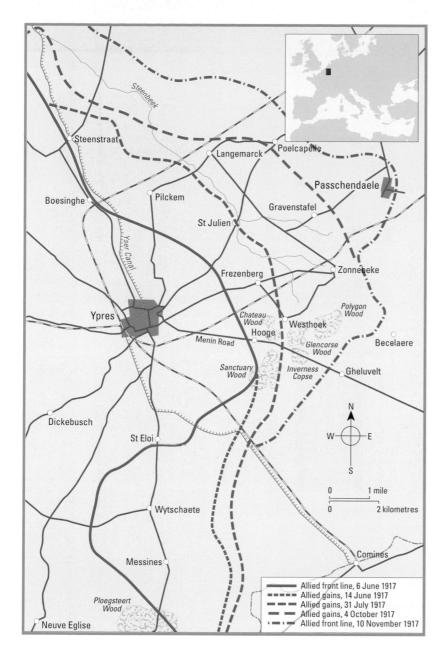

The Third Battle of Ypres, 1917.
British soldiers commonly named
it after the small, smashed
village they eventually managed
to capture – Passchendaele.

US President Woodrow Wilson
led his country into the war in
April 1917.

this information reached the US
government, war with Germany
was inevitable.

Although US naval forces made
an immediate difference in the
Atlantic, on land the US
intervention had no immediate
impact. Its army was tiny and
inefficient, and it was almost
eighteen months before a large
modern force could be raised,
equipped, trained, and brought to

bear on the enemy. In the
meantime, the British made one
last effort to win the war on their
own.

Haig had spent eighteen
months planning his Ypres
offensive of July 1917. The
Germans had spent almost as long
preparing to meet it. The result
was a titanic struggle akin to that
which had taken place at Verdun
the previous year. No breakthrough

came, although the British did
manage to take the high ground
that overlooked Ypres, including
the village of Passchendaele.
However, the 310,000 casualties
that it cost hurt the British much
as the French had been hurt the
previous spring.

## THE COLLAPSE OF
## RUSSIA By unwisely assuming
overall command on the Eastern
Front in September 1915, Tsar
Nicholas II of Russia sealed his
own fate. Henceforward all failures

– and there were many – would ultimately be laid his feet. By the end of 1916 the country's railway system had collapsed, and millions of city-dwellers faced starvation. The armed forces were in chaos. The tsar and his government were thoroughly discredited.

Food riots in March 1917 brought matters to a head. The tsar abdicated and was replaced by a Western-style republican government that promised to hold free elections. It did not, however, take Russia out of the war. In July 1917, at the request of his hard-pressed allies in the west, Prime Minister Alexander Kerensky called for yet another offensive. It lasted nineteen days. Faced with fierce counterattacks by the Central Powers, along broad stretches of the front the Russian soldiers simply threw down their arms and fled. A further German offensive in September pushed closer to Petrograd (St Petersburg).

Kerensky's unelected Provisional Government staggered on until November, when it was overthrown in a communist coup in Petrograd.

**The collapse of Russia on the Eastern Front, 1917-18. The German advance brought them vast industrial and agricultural wealth.**

## THE TREATY OF BREST-LITOVSK

Russia surrendered the following to the Central Powers:

| | |
|---|---|
| Territory | Ukraine, Finland, Baltic Provinces (Estonia, Lithuania, Latvia), the Caucasus, Belorussia (White Russia), Poland. |
| Population | 33 per cent |
| Railway network | 53 per cent |
| Arable land | 25 per cent |
| Coal fields | 70 per cent |
| Total industry | 40 per cent |

Trotsky hoped the communist revolution would spread from Russia to Germany and other countries, so he put off reaching an agreement with the Germans. They responded by advancing rapidly towards Petrograd. This forced Trotsky's hand. On 3 March 1918 Russia formally made peace, surrendering to the Germans vast territories, including the Ukraine, Finland and Poland, and much of its industrial capacity. Germany was now free to concentrate all its resources on the Western Front in an attempt to win the war before American power could make itself felt.

**Trotsky and Stalin, key members of the communist Bolshevik party, address crowds of supporters in Moscow, October 1917.**

The communists rapidly extended their rule to Moscow and other cities, attracting support with their slogan, 'Peace! Bread! Land!' To provide the promised peace, the country's new leaders, Vladimir Lenin and Foreign Minister Leon Trotsky, signed an armistice with the Germans on 3 December 1917. Negotiations soon followed.

**Alexander Kerensky, Russia's liberal premier who alienated his countrymen by continuing the war with Germany.**

# CHAPTER 4:
# VICTORY AND DEFEAT

General Erich von Ludendorff, the German commander who masterminded his country's final offensive in the spring of 1918. He is pictured here after the war in around 1924.

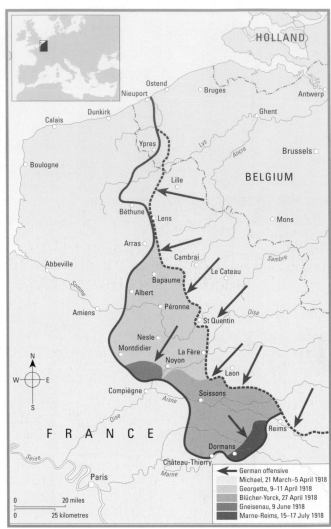

Germany's spring offensives, 1918. A series of dramatic offensives in early 1918 managed to recapture in weeks territory that had been lost over the previous years.

The final German offensives that would win or lose the war were masterminded by General Erich von Ludendorff. For this first attack, and the one about which he was most optimistic, he chose his ground carefully. His target was the lightly-held British front on the old Somme battlefield, perhaps the weakest point in the enemy line. By mid-March he had transferred thousands of troops from the Eastern Front, assembling three German armies (sixty-three divisions or some 630,000 men) to face twenty-six divisions of the British Third and Fifth Armies.

The German assault began in thick fog on 21 March. First came a 6,000-gun bombardment, many firing mustard gas shells, then an advance all along the line. Overwhelmed, the British fell back. For a time it looked as if the two armies might be split apart, leaving the Germans free to sweep into the heart of France. To cope with the crisis, the French soldier Marshal Ferdinand Foch was appointed supreme commander of all Allied forces on the Western Front. Co-ordinating the resistance, he rushed French reinforcements to the front. Finally, having fallen back eighty kilometres in places (the greatest movement of the trench war), the Allied line held fast. On 5 April Ludendorff called the operation off.

## THE COST OF THE LUDENDORFF OFFENSIVES, MARCH–JUNE 1918

**Casualties (killed and wounded)**

| | German | French | British | Total |
|---|---|---|---|---|
| Somme/Lys | 348,000 | 112,000 | 343,000 | 803,000 |
| Aisne | 130,000 | 96,000 | 28,000 | 254,000 |
| Oise | 45,000 | 35,000 | | 80,000 |
| **Total killed in four offensives** | 124,000 | 220,000 | 61,000 | 405,000 |

One of many thousands of British soldiers killed during the German offensives of 1918. This man died covering the retreat of his comrades.

Having failed to break through on the Somme, Ludendorff turned his attention to the line further north. Here he had located another weakly-defended British sector, this time south of Ypres on the River Lys. Launching another gigantic attack, the Germans came extremely close to breaking through. Indeed, if Ludendorff had been less cautious in following up early progress, the Lys Offensive (9–29 April) might have led to a German victory.

Abandoning the Lys offensive, Ludendorff turned his attention to the French on the River Aisne (27 May–2 June) and in the Oise Valley (Noyon-Montdidier, 9 to 13 June). As before, neither offensive made the anticipated progress. Despite suffering enormous casualties, the Allied line remained intact. Ludendorff's time was running out.

### ALLIED ADVANCE

Ludendorff next planned a huge summer offensive for the Flanders

The Frenchman Marshal Ferdinand Foch was given overall command of the Allies on the Western Front in 1918.

**Blinded by an attack with poison gas during the Second Battle of the Marne (July 1918), two French soldiers are led to a field hospital by their comrades.**

region, where the line was held by the British and Belgians. To tie down the French and prevent them from sending reinforcements north, on 15 July 1918 he launched an attack along the River Marne. Here, on the site of the first major battle of the war, three German armies advanced on either side of the famous Champagne city of Reims (see page 29).

A familiar pattern emerged. The Germans made some progress but were halted when the Allies managed to bring up reinforcements. On this occasion, however, the fighting did not stop there. To the Germans' surprise, on 18 July Foch ordered a counterattack. Backed by 350 tanks, the French drove the Germans back over the ground they had captured and beyond. Ludendorff urgently brought up reinforcements of his own and had stopped the Allied advance by early August. Nevertheless, an attack had become a serious defeat, and plans for a further German offensive were cancelled.

It was now the turn of the Allies to go on the offensive. Putting into effect Haig's plan, Foch's first aim was to eliminate the salients in the Allied line that

---

### CROSSING THE OLD BATTLEFIELD

In the autumn of 1918 Major P.H. Pilditch cycled across the Somme battlefield searching for the grave of a friend killed in 1914:

*'On the way back we spent some time in the old No Man's Land of four years' duration … It was a morbid but intensely interesting occupation tracing the various battles among the hundreds of skulls, bones and remains scattered thickly about. The progress of our successive attacks could be clearly seen from the types of equipment on the skeletons, soft caps denoting 1914 and early 1915, then respirators, then steel helmets marking attacks in 1916. … There were many of these poor remains all along the German wire.'*

[Quoted in *The Imperial War Museum Book of the First World War*, edited by Malcolm Brown]

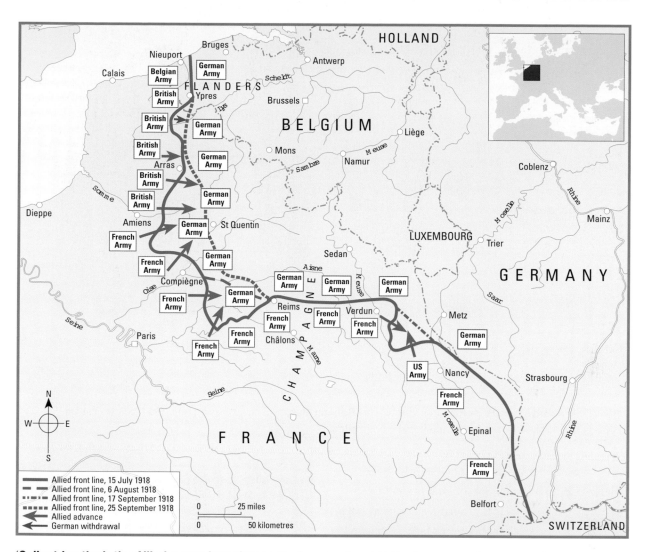

**'Salient busting': the Allied campaigns that pushed back the Germans and reduced the salients (bulges) in the front line on the Western Front, July-September 1918.**

had been created by the Ludendorff offensives. By 5 August the Aisne salient had been recovered. Then, on 8 August, a large-scale attack was launched to the east of Amiens to recapture the lost Somme battlefield. On a remarkable first day – the 'black day of the German army' – British, French and Canadian troops advanced 16 km. Six thousand prisoners were taken and 100 guns captured. In some places the Germans, for the first time in the war, fled in disarray before the overwhelming onslaught of tanks, aircraft, artillery and infantry.

**Some of the many thousands of German soldiers captured by the Allies during August 1918.**

The Allies pressed forward until early September, by which time the Germans had abandoned all the ground gained earlier and withdrawn to the Hindenburg Line. Thousands more prisoners had been taken and many more guns seized. As summer turned to autumn, the outlook for the German Army was looking bleaker by the day.

**IMPACT OF AMERICA** Having entered the war in April 1917, General John Pershing, the commander of the US forces in France (the American Expeditionary Force, AEF) set about building an American Army. By the end of the war there were some two million US troops in France, where they were trained and equipped.

First to see action was the US First Division, which on 28 May 1918

| AMERICAN CASUALTIES ON THE WESTERN FRONT | |
| --- | --- |
| Cantigny | 1,600 |
| Belleau Wood | 8,800 |
| Marne | 40,000 |
| St Mihiel | 7,000 |
| Meuse-Argonne | 117,000 |
| **Total in all theatres 281,000** | |

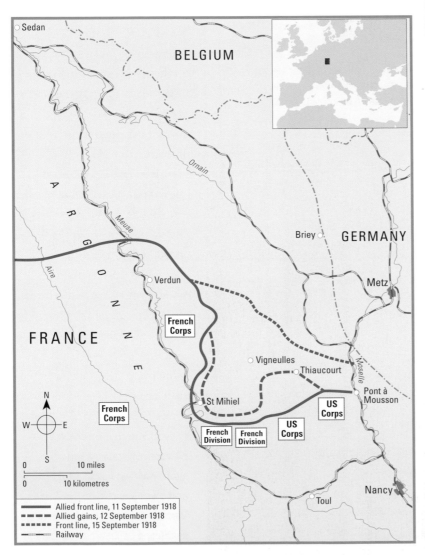

Enter the USA – the St Mihiel battlefield where American forces made their first major contribution to the Allied victory.

US troops of the 18th Infantry Machine Gun Battalion advance towards the front line near St Mihiel, 13 September 1918.

successfully captured the village of Cantigny during the German Aisne River offensive. A week later the Second Division withstood a German attack and captured Belleau Wood near Château-Thierry. By the time of the Marne attack and counterattack (see pages 44-45), the US had over a quarter of a million men in the field. The American First Army, however, was not ready for independent action until the end of the month.

The full impact of the US intervention was finally felt in September, during the Allied salient-busting operations. The US First Army was given the task of reducing the St Mihiel salient south-east of Verdun. Attacking on 12 September with 600 aircraft in support, the Americans caught the Germans in the process of withdrawing and cleared most of the salient in a single day. The message to the Allies and foe alike was obvious – the Americans were now a force to be reckoned with.

From St Mihiel Pershing moved north of Verdun to work with the French in the massive Meuse-Argonne offensive that lasted to the end of the war (see pages 48-49). After good progress when the attack began, the Americans became bogged down in October and suffered heavy casualties. With more and more troops ready for battle each day, the AEF was now divided into two armies. By the time of the Armistice on 11 November, they were once again making rapid progress, and even beat the French in the 'race to Sedan'. As many had predicted in 1917, once the US had managed to mobilize its manpower all hopes of a German victory had disappeared.

The transatlantic alliance – US General John Pershing (right), the commander of the American Expeditionary Force, with the Allied commander-in-chief Marshal Foch of France.

# CHAPTER 5:
# THE END OF THE WAR

Armistice at last. Joyful Parisians celebrate the end of hostilities on the streets of the French capital on 11 November 1918.

## THE FINISH OF THE WAR

British soldier James Bird wrote home describing the day the war stopped.

'The Saturday afternoon was very exciting, the band of the Canadians played in the square, and during the afternoon two of our planes did all sorts of tricks and stunts, flying very low, this simply made the inhabitants go mad with delight …

[Monday.] This was the day of the finish of the war. I walked into Mons in the afternoon, we were mobbed and nearly lost all our buttons. It was indeed a great day for Britain, as well as France. It made one feel glad to be alive, and to think that after four years hard fighting we had at last reached the place where our troops were in 1914 …'

[Quoted in *The Imperial War Museum Book of the First World War*, edited by Malcolm Brown]

**H**aving removed the dangerous salients from their line, on 26 September the Allies began their final onslaught. Foch's master plan involved three offensives: a small Belgian attack forward of Ypres, larger forces of French and Americans in a pincer movement on the River Meuse swinging north of Verdun, and the British and French, in the largest attack, driving towards Cambrai and St Quentin.

The southern Franco-American offensive was the first to begin. With overwhelming force, including air

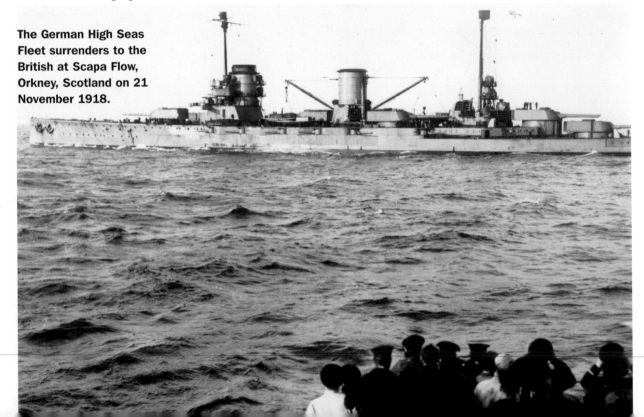

The German High Seas Fleet surrenders to the British at Scapa Flow, Orkney, Scotland on 21 November 1918.

superiority and large contingents of tanks, the Allies drove the Germans steadily back, capturing Sedan on 6 November. The armistice was signed as they prepared to move south over the German border to Metz.

At the other end of the line the Belgians (with some support from other nations) advanced equally rapidly to Ostend and on towards Antwerp. To their south the British, supported by French and American divisions, took Cambrai, forced the Germans to abandon the Hindenburg Line on 4 October, and were pushing on towards Charleroi when hostilities ceased.

Hindenburg and Ludendorff had been virtually running Germany since early 1918. When their armies were pushed back so dramatically in the autumn, Ludendorff put out feelers for a ceasefire. The terms were unacceptable – Germany was asked to surrender all land occupied since 1870, dismantle its armed forces, surrender much of its martial equipment, and set aside its treaties with Russia and Romania.

As the war dragged on, Germany's allies began to desert. Bulgaria signed an armistice on 29 September. At home mounting starvation and discontent led to strikes and riots. When the navy mutinied, revolution became a real possibility. Ludendorff accepted the inevitable. On 26 October he resigned and fled to Sweden. Hindenburg remained at his post. Turkey signed an armistice on 30 October, and Austria-Hungary on 3 November. Finally, at 11 am on 11 November, Germany too accepted the Allies' terms and the guns finally fell silent.

**The final Allied advance, autumn 1918. After the war the Germans took pride in the fact that no foreign soldier had set foot on their soil.**

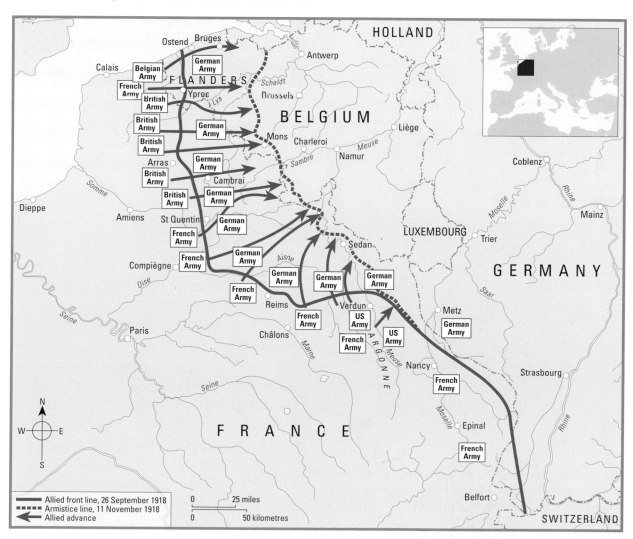

**MAKING PEACE** A series of long-negotiated treaties turned the various short-term armistices into what was hoped would be lasting peace. The Treaty of St Germain organized the break-up of the Austro-Hungarian Empire, creating the separate states of Austria, Hungary, and Czechoslovakia (the Balkan peoples had already established themselves as Yugoslavia). As with the other treaties, it also limited the military capacity of the former Central Powers. At Neuilly (27 November 1919) Bulgaria's frontiers were established. The terms of Hungary's surrender were sealed at Trianon on 4 June 1920. The Treaty of Trianon (10 August 1920) broke up the Ottoman Empire, leaving the much smaller state of Turkey.

By far the most important treaty was that dealing with Germany. Signed at Versailles, France, on 28 June 1919, it was an extremely harsh document that the

Germans had no option but to accept. This was not what some peacemakers had envisaged in 1918. For instance, in his Fourteen Points (January 1918), US President Woodrow Wilson had set out a reasonable and moderate set of peace aims. At Versailles these were overridden by the demands of French Prime Minister Georges Clemenceau and, to a lesser extent, British Prime Minister David Lloyd George. Both were driven by public opinion at home demanding vengeance after four-and-a-half years of slaughter.

By the Treaty of Versailles Germany lost all its colonies and some territory in Europe. It was obliged to accept total responsibility for the war, disband most of its armed forces, and pay the Allies an impossible 200 million gold marks (£6,600 million) in reparations [compensation] for war damage. Britain and France also took possession of the former Central Powers' colonies. As the popular cry ran, Germany had been squeezed 'until the pips squeaked'.

As many recognized at the time, the Versailles settlement was no recipe for long-term peace. It left the once proud Germany humiliated, weakened and impoverished – ideal soil in which extremists might plant their wicked seeds of revenge. In this way the ground was prepared for World War II, which broke out just over twenty years after the end of this 'War to End All Wars',

## WHAT MIGHT HAVE BEEN ...

In introducing his Fourteen Points to the US Congress on 8 January 1918, President Wilson spoke of the world he hoped would emerge after the war:

*'What we demand in this war ... is that the world be made fit and safe to live in; and particularly that it be made safe for every peace-loving nation which, like our own, wishes to live its own life, determine its own institutions, be assured of justice and fair dealings by the other peoples of the world, as against force and selfish aggression. All the peoples of the world are in effect partners in this interest ...'*

[Quoted in *Great Issues in American History: From Reconstruction to the Present Day, 1864-1969*, edited by Richard Hofstadter]

**(Left to right) Prime Minister David Lloyd George of Great Britain, President Georges Clemenceau of France and US President Woodrow Wilson on their way to the Versailles peace talks, June 1919.**

Post-war Europe, showing the much reduced Austria, Germany, Russia and Turkey, and the host of new states, such as Czechoslovakia and Yugoslavia. Danzig was termed a Free City under League of Nations protection.

Into the Roaring Twenties – thousands of delighted citizens turn out for a victory parade on New York's Fifth Avenue, 1919.

# PROFILES OF MILITARY AND POLITICAL LEADERS

## THE GENERALS

### GENERAL ALEXEI BRUSILOV (1853-1926)

Unlike most World War I commanders, the energetic Alexei Brusilov showed both flair and imagination. Having made a name for himself in Russia's war with Turkey, 1877-8, he was key to his country's advance into Galicia in 1914. His finest moment was the spectacular but ultimately unsuccessful offensive of 1916 which greatly helped his hard-pressed French allies on the Western Front. After the war he served with the communist Red Army.

### MARSHAL FERDINAND FOCH (1851-1929)

Having lived under occupation in Lorraine, a province that France had surrendered to Germany after military defeat in 1871, Ferdinand Foch needed no motivation in his quest to drive out the invader. An author of two books on strategy, he distinguished himself at the Battle of the Marne (1914). For much of the war he had called for all Allied forces to be under a single command. When the idea finally became reality in 1918, the task fell to him. Showing great skill, insight

and tact, he masterminded the successful Allied offensives of the final months of the war.

### FIELD MARSHAL DOUGLAS HAIG (1861-1928)

Douglas Haig is one of the most controversial military commanders in British history. His supporters refer to his steely character, his determination to succeed against all odds (a man of powerful faith, he seemed to have believed that God was guiding him), and his skilful offensives of 1918. Opponents accuse him of being rigid in strategy and insensitive to human losses, particularly during the British Somme, Arras, and Passchendaele offensives, 1916-17.

### FIELD MARSHAL PAUL VON HINDENBURG (1847-1934)

The aristocratic Paul von Hindenburg went to army cadet school at the age of eleven and served with distinction until retirement in 1911. On the

outbreak of war, he was recalled and sent, with the more able second-in-command Ludendorff, to meet the Russian attack on Prussia. His reputation was made by victories at Tannenberg and Masurian Lakes. Placed in overall command of Central Powers strategy in 1916, he concentrated, unsuccessfully, on defence. He was elected president of Germany in 1925, and appointed Adolf Hitler chancellor in 1933.

### GENERAL FRANZ CONRAD VON HOTZENDORF (1852-1925)

Having been put in charge of the Austrian Army in 1906, Franz Conrad was eager for war with Serbia and Italy. When war came, however, he found it more testing than he expected, especially against Serbia. In the end, his most likely chance of success – against Italy in 1916 – was cut short by the Brusilov Offensive. He was put under Hindenburg's overall command in September 1916 and dismissed the following year.

### MUSTAFA KEMAL (1881-1938)

Known in later life as the 'father of the Turks' (Ataturk), Kemal played a vital role in resisting the Allied landings in Gallipoli in 1916. He then fought with distinction in the Caucasus, remaining the only undefeated Turkish commander. First president of the new Turkish Republic (1924), he crowned his military career with an even more successful one as a modernizing politician.

### GENERAL ERICH VON LUDENDORFF (1865-1937)

Extremely able but occasionally flawed in judgement, von Ludendorff helped re-arrange the Schlieffen Plan (see pages 6-7) and guided Hindenburg in the key victories against Russia in 1914. Thereafter, Hindenburg and Ludendorff worked closely together, becoming virtual masters of Germany by 1918. Having almost won the war with his Spring 1918 offensives, Ludendorff's fortunes declined rapidly. He fled to Sweden in disguise in 1918, re-emerging after the war as a Nazi politician.

### GENERAL HELMUTH VON MOLTKE (1848-1916)

Nephew of one of Prussia's greatest generals, Helmuth von Moltke (sometimes known as 'von Moltke the Younger') is principally remembered for working with Ludendorff to alter the Schlieffen Plan to attack western France. By weakening the German right flank, which was to sweep down to the west of Paris, he was partly responsible for the failure of the German strategy at the Battle of the Marne, 1914. He was dismissed two days later.

### GENERAL JOHN JOSEPH PERSHING (1860-1948)

John Pershing's military experience, gained in small-scale encounters

such as chasing bandits in Mexico, hardly fitted him for what he was to meet on the Western Front. However, appointed to command the AEF in 1917, he built it up into an effective fighting force. Although Clemenceau called for his dismissal after a poor showing in the Argonne Forest, the idea was rejected and Pershing's armies played an important part in the Allies' last offensives of 1918.

### MARSHAL PHILIPPE PÉTAIN (1856-1951)

Philippe Pétain, a keen student of war, realized earlier than most experts that offensives against artillery, barbed wire, and machine guns would be virtually impossible. His advice was ignored. Not until the Germans threatened breakthrough at Verdun in February 1917 did he get the chance to put his ideas to the test. The dramatic defence of Verdun made him a national hero, and he was made commander-in-chief of the French Army in May 1917. Tragically, the 'hero of Verdun' ended his life in prison for treacherous co-operation with the Nazis in World War II.

## THE POLITICIANS

### GEORGES CLEMENCEAU (1841-1929)

French Prime Minister
A tough and energetic man of peasant stock, the seventy-six-year-old Clemenceau (nicknamed 'the Tiger') took over the leadership of France in the grim days of 1917. His speeches and single-minded dedication lifted the nation, and guided it to victory the following year. A keen admirer of the USA, he was always eager for it to join the Allies.

### DAVID LLOYD GEORGE (1863-1945)

British Prime Minister
Lloyd George had doubts about

going to war, but changed his mind after the German invasion of Belgium. Thereafter, as Minister of Munitions and Prime Minister (December 1916 onwards), he used his considerable skills to gear the nation's industrial might to winning the war. As a radical, he did not always see eye to eye with high-born military commanders.

### NICHOLAS II (1868-1918)

Tsar of Russia
Russia could hardly have had a less suitable leader during World War I. Nicholas, the hereditary tsar, was blessed with neither intelligence, nor steadfastness, nor insight. He chose poor ministers and generals, and allowed his court to become a nest of scandal. Having abdicated in 1917, he and his family were executed by the communists the following year.

### WILHELM II (1859-1941)

Emperor of Germany
Rather out of his depth in the world of international politics into which he had been born, on several occasions Wilhelm II (emperor or kaiser from 1888 onwards) upset relations with Britain through his tactless statements and actions. Having offered to support Austria-Hungary against Serbia in 1914, thereby making war likely, his influence declined. He abdicated on 9 November 1918 and fled the country.

### WOODROW WILSON (1856-1924)

In some ways the most attractive of the war leaders, the idealistic Wilson worked as an academic before being elected US president in 1912. He reluctantly took his country to war in 1917, then worked tirelessly for a better world once victory had been achieved. Sadly, having moderated his allies' calls for vengeance at Versailles, illness prevented him from taking his plans further.

STIRLING COUNCIL LIBRARIES

# STATISTICS CONCERNING COMBATANT NATIONS

All statistics taken from John Ellis and Michael Cox, eds., *The World War I Databook*, Aurum Press, 1993.

## AGGREGATE MILITARY CASUALTIES AND CIVILIAN DEATHS OF THE BELLIGERENTS 1914-18

| Country | Population (millions) | Number Served in Forces (millions) | Force Casualties | | | | |
| --- | --- | --- | --- | --- | --- | --- | --- |
| | | | Killed and Missing | Wounded | P.O.W. | Total Killed, Wounded & Missing | Total Civilian Deaths |
| Australia | 4.87 | 0.42 | 53,560 | 155,130 | 3,650 | 208,690 | – |
| Austria-Hungary | 49.90 | 7.80 | 539,630 | 1,943,240 | 2,118,190 | 2,482,870 | ? |
| Belgium | 7.52 | 0.27 | 38,170 | 44,690 | 10,200 | 82,860 | 30,000 |
| Bulgaria | 5.50 | 1.20 | 77,450 | 152,400 | 10,620 | 229,850 | 275,000 |
| Canada | 7.40 | 0.62 | 58,990 | 149,710 | 2,820 | 208,700 | – |
| France | 39.60 | 8.66 | 1,385,300 | 4,329,200 | 446,300 | 5,714,500 | 40,000 |
| Germany | 67.00 | 13.40 | 2,037,000 | 5,687,000 | 993,800 | 7,724,000 | 700,000 |
| Greece | 4.80 | 0.28 | 5,000 | 20,000 | c.1,000 | 25,000 | 130,000 |
| India | 316.00 | 1.68 | 62,060 | 66,690 | 11,070 | 128,750 | – |
| Italy | 35.00 | 5.90 | 462,400 | 955,000 | 530,000 | 1,417,400 | ? |
| Japan | 67.20 | 0.80 | ? | ? | – | 1,970 | – |
| New Zealand | 1.05 | 0.13 | 16,710 | 41,320 | 500 | 58,030 | – |
| Portugal | 6.00 | 0.20 | 7,220 | 13,751 | 6,680 | 20,971 | – |
| Romania | 7.51 | ? | 219,800 | 120,000 | c.60,000 | 339,800 | 265,000 to 500,000 |
| Russia | 167.00 | 12.00 | 1,800,000 | 4,950,000 | 3,910,000 | 6,750,000 | 2,000,000 |
| Serbia | 5.00 | 0.71 | 127,500 | 133,150 | 70,000 | 260,650 | 600,000 |
| South Africa | 6.00 | 0.23 | 7,120 | 12,030 | 1,540 | 19,150 | ? |
| Turkey | 21.30 | 0.99 | 236,000 | 770,000 | 145,000 | 1,006,000 | 2,000,000 |
| United Kingdom | 46.40 | 5.70 | 702,410 | 1,662,625 | 170,389 | 2,365,035 | 1,386 |
| United States | 92.00 | 4.35 | 51,822 | 230,074 | 4,434 | 281,896 | – |

## AGGREGATE NAVAL LOSSES OF THE MAJOR POWERS, BY TYPE OF SHIP, AND AGGREGATE PERSONNEL LOSSES 1914-18

| | UK | France | Russia | Italy | Japan | USA | Total | Germany | Austria-Hungary | Turkey | Total |
| --- | --- | --- | --- | --- | --- | --- | --- | --- | --- | --- | --- |
| Battleship | 13 | 4 | 2 | 3 | 1 | – | 23 | 1 | 3 | 2 | 6 |
| Battlecruiser | 3 | – | – | – | 1 | – | 4 | 1 | – | – | 1 |
| Cruiser | 13 | 5 | 2 | 3 | – | 1 | 24 | 6 | 2 | 1 | 9 |
| Light Cruiser | 12 | – | 1 | – | 2 | – | 15 | 18 | – | – | 18 |
| Monitor | 5 | – | – | 2 | – | – | 7 | – | 3 | – | 3 |
| Torpedo Gunboat | 5 | 3 | – | – | – | – | 8 | – | – | – | – |
| Sloop | 18 | – | 3 | – | – | – | 21 | – | – | 9 | 9 |
| Destroyer | 67 | 15 | 6 | 8 | 1 | 2 | 99 | }109 | 6 | 1 | }126 |
| Torpedo Boat | 11 | 10 | 9 | 4 | 1 | – | 35 | | 8 | 2 | |
| Aircraft Carrier | 3 | – | – | – | – | – | 3 | – | – | – | – |
| Minelayer | 2 | 2 | 5 | – | – | – | 9 | – | – | 1 | 1 |
| Minesweeper | – | – | 30 | 2 | – | 1 | 33 | 29 | – | 2 | 31 |

| | UK | France | Russia | Italy | Japan | USA | Total | Germany | A-Hungary | Turkey | Total |
|---|---|---|---|---|---|---|---|---|---|---|---|
| Submarine | 54 | 14 | 12 | 11 | – | – | 91 | 178 | 7 | – | 185 |
| **Personnel:** | | | | | | | | | | | |
| killed | 34,650 | 15,650 | ? | 3,170 | ? | 8,106 | ? | 78,300 | 980 | ? | ? |
| wounded | 4,510 | | ? | 5,250 | ? | | ? | | 310 | ? | ? |

## ANNUAL GERMAN U-BOAT LOSSES BY LOCALITY 1914-18

| | North Sea, Orkneys and Shetlands | English Channel and Belgian Coast | North Channel, Irish Sea, Bristol Channel | North Atlantic | South Atlantic (south of Scilly Isles) | Baltic | Mediterranean | Black Sea and Bosphorous | Unknown | Total |
|---|---|---|---|---|---|---|---|---|---|---|
| 1914 | 3 | 2 | – | – | – | – | – | – | – | 5 |
| 1915 | 10 | 2 | 1 | 1 | 2 | 1 | – | 1 | 1 | 19 |
| 1916 | 8 | 2 | 1 | 4 | – | 1 | 1 | 3 | 2 | 22 |
| 1917 | 13 | 13 | 4 | 25 | 5 | 1 | 2 | – | – | 63 |
| 1918 | 13 | 9 | 9 | 14 | 10 | – | 12 | – | 2 | 69 |
| Total | 47 | 28 | 15 | 44 | 17 | 3 | 15 | 4 | 5 | 178 |

## MONTHLY TOTALS OF BRITISH, ALLIED AND NEUTRAL MERCHANT SHIPPING LOST THROUGH ENEMY ACTION 1914-18 (GROSS TONNAGE)

| | British | Allied and Neutral | Total |
|---|---|---|---|
| 1914 August | 44,692 | 18,075 | 62,767 |
| 1914 September | 89,251 | 9,127 | 98,378 |
| 1914 October | 78,088 | 9,829 | 87,917 |
| 1914 November | 9,348 | 10,065 | 19,413 |
| 1914 December | 26,815 | 17,382 | 44,197 |
| **TOTAL** | **248,194** | **64,478** | **312,672** |
| | | | |
| 1915 January | 32,276 | 15,705 | 47,981 |
| 1915 February | 36,372 | 23,549 | 59,921 |
| 1915 March | 71,768 | 9,007 | 80,775 |
| 1915 April | 24,383 | 31,342 | 55,725 |
| 1915 May | 89,673 | 30,385 | 120,058 |
| 1915 June | 91,315 | 40,113 | 131,428 |
| 1915 July | 57,274 | 52,366 | 109,640 |
| 1915 August | 151,354 | 34,512 | 185,866 |
| 1915 September | 102,135 | 49,749 | 151,884 |
| 1915 October | 54,156 | 34,378 | 88,534 |
| 1915 November | 94,655 | 58,388 | 153,043 |
| 1915 December | 74,490 | 48,651 | 123,141 |
| **TOTAL** | **879,851** | **428,145** | **1,307,996** |
| | | | |
| 1916 January | 62,645 | 18,614 | 81,259 |
| 1916 February | 75,928 | 41,619 | 117,547 |
| 1916 March | 99,696 | 67,401 | 167,097 |
| 1916 April | 141,409 | 50,258 | 191,667 |
| 1916 May | 64,722 | 64,453 | 129,175 |
| 1916 June | 36,976 | 71,879 | 108,855 |
| 1916 July | 85,228 | 32,987 | 118,215 |
| 1916 August | 45,026 | 117,718 | 162,744 |
| 1916 September | 109,263 | 121,197 | 230,460 |
| 1916 October | 177,386 | 176,274 | 353,660 |

| | British | Allied and Neutral | Total |
|---|---|---|---|
| 1916 November | 170,409 | 141,099 | 311,508 |
| 1916 December | 182,728 | 172,411 | 355,139 |
| **TOTAL** | **1,251,416** | **1,075,910** | **2,327,326** |
| | | | |
| 1917 January | 155,686 | 212,835 | 368,521 |
| 1917 February | 316,964 | 223,042 | 540,006 |
| 1917 March | 357,064 | 236,777 | 593,841 |
| 1917 April | 551,202 | 329,825 | 881,027 |
| 1917 May | 353,737 | 242,892 | 596,629 |
| 1917 June | 419,267 | 268,240 | 687,507 |
| 1917 July | 367,594 | 190,394 | 557,988 |
| 1917 August | 330,052 | 181,678 | 511,730 |
| 1917 September | 196,457 | 155,291 | 351,748 |
| 1917 October | 276,359 | 182,199 | 458,558 |
| 1917 November | 173,647 | 115,565 | 289,212 |
| 1917 December | 253,500 | 145,611 | 399,111 |
| **TOTAL** | **3,751,529** | **2,484,349** | **6,235,878** |
| | | | |
| 1918 January | 180,348 | 126,310 | 306,658 |
| 1918 February | 227,582 | 91,375 | 318,957 |
| 1918 March | 199,751 | 142,846 | 342,597 |
| 1918 April | 215,784 | 62,935 | 278,719 |
| 1918 May | 192,938 | 102,582 | 295,520 |
| 1918 June | 163,629 | 91,958 | 255,587 |
| 1918 July | 166,004 | 130,963 | 296,967 |
| 1918 August | 147,257 | 136,558 | 283,815 |
| 1918 September | 137,001 | 50,880 | 187,881 |
| 1918 October | 59,229 | 59,330 | 118,559 |
| 1918 November | 10,220 | 7,462 | 17,682 |
| **TOTAL** | **1,699,743** | **1,003,199** | **2,666,942** |
| | | | |
| **GRAND TOTAL** | **7,830,733** | **5,056,081** | **12,886,814** |

# SIGNIFICANT DATES

**1830**
Greece gains independence from the Turkish Empire.

**1839**
Treaty of London guarantees the neutrality of Belgium.

**1859-70**
Kingdom of Italy created.

**1861**
Romania formed.

**1870-1**
Franco-Prussian War.

**JANUARY 1871**
German Empire proclaimed at Versailles.

**MAY 1871**
Treaty of Paris. France cedes Alsace and Lorraine to Germany.

**1878**
Congress of Berlin. Serbia, Bosnia-Herzegovina, Bulgaria, Montenegro and Romania granted independence from Turkey.

**1879**
Austro-German Dual Alliance.

**1882**
Italy agrees Triple Alliance with Germany and Austria-Hungary.

**1888**
Wilhelm II becomes Kaiser (emperor) of Germany.

**1894**
Franco-Russian Alliance signed.

**1898**
Germany begins its naval build-up.

**1902**
Anglo-Japanese Alliance.

**1904**
Anglo-French *entente cordiale*.

**1905**
Schlieffen Plan drawn up.

**1907**
British Expeditionary Force formed.
Anglo-Russian entente.

**1908**
Austria-Hungary annexes Bosnia and Herzegovina.

**1912**
Woodrow Wilson elected president of the USA.

**1912-3**
Two Balkan Wars.

**JANUARY 1914**
German officer commands Constantinople garrison.

**28 JUNE 1914**
Archduke Franz Ferdinand assassinated in Sarajevo, Bosnia.

**28 JULY 1914**
Austria-Hungary declares war on Serbia. Russia mobilizes.

**1 AUGUST 1914**
Germany declares war on Russia. France mobilizes.

**3 AUGUST 1914**
Germany declares war on France.

**4 AUGUST 1914**
German troops enter Belgium. (Midnight) Britain declares war on Germany.

**12 AUGUST 1914**
Britain and France declare war on Austria-Hungary.

**23 AUGUST 1914**
Japan joins Allies.

**26-30 AUGUST 1914**
Germans defeat Russians at Tannenberg (above).

**5-9 SEPTEMBER 1914**
German advance on the Western Front stopped at the Battle of the Marne.

**9-14 SEPTEMBER 1914**
Germans defeat Russians at Masurian Lakes.

**14 SEPTEMBER 1914**
Falkenhayn becomes German commander-in-chief.

**29 OCTOBER 1914**
Turkey joins Central Powers.

**30 OCTOBER-4 NOVEMBER 1914**
First Battle of Ypres.

**NOVEMBER 1914**
Russian advances in Galicia.

**29 DECEMBER 1914-3 JANUARY 1915**
Russians defeat Turks at Sarikamish.

**FEBRUARY 1915**
Germany begins unrestricted submarine warfare (to September). Allied naval forces fail to pass through the Dardanelles.

**MARCH 1915**
Allied offensive at Neuve-Chapelle.

**25 APRIL 1915**
Allies land at Gallipoli.

**APRIL-MAY 1915**
2nd Battle of Ypres – first use of poison gas.

**MAY 1915**
Italy joins Allies.
Allied offensive in Artois.
Germans making gains on Eastern Front.

**AUGUST 1915**
Germans capture Warsaw (Poland).
Nicholas II takes command of Russian armies.

**SEPTEMBER 1915**
French offensive in Champagne.
Allied Artois-Loos offensive (to November).
Bulgaria joins Central Powers.
Serbia overwhelmed.

**OCTOBER 1915**
Allies land at Salonika in Greece.

**DECEMBER 1915**
Joffre becomes French commander-in-chief. Haig becomes British commander in chief.

**21 FEBRUARY 1916**
German attack on Verdun begins (to December). Pétain ordered to defend Verdun.

**31 MAY-1 JUNE 1916**
Battle of Jutland (foot of page).

**4 JUNE 1916**
Brusilov offensive begins (to September).

**1 JULY 1916**
British Somme offensive begins (to November) (right).

**AUGUST 1916**
Romania joins Allies.
Hindenburg replaces Falkenhayn as German commander-in-chief.

**DECEMBER 1916**
Lloyd George becomes British prime minister.
Nivelle becomes French commander-in-chief.

**JANUARY 1917**
Zimmerman telegram urging Mexico to attack United States in alliance with Germany intercepted.

**FEBRUARY 1917**
Germans begin to fall back to Hindenburg Line. Germany reintroduces unrestricted submarine warfare.

**MARCH 1917**
Nicholas II abdicates after revolution in Russia.
British take Baghdad in Mesopotamia.

**6 APRIL 1917**
USA declares war on Germany.

**9 APRIL-16 MAY 1917**
British offensive at Arras.

**16 APRIL-9 MAY 1917**
Nivelle's disastrous offensive on River Aisne.

**MAY 1917**
Allies introduce convoys to protect merchant shipping.
Pétain becomes French commander-in-chief.

**JUNE 1917**
First US troops land in France.

**JULY 1917**
Kerensky offensive on Eastern Front.

**31 JULY 1917**
Third Battle of Ypres (Passchendaele) begins (to November).

**SEPTEMBER 1917**
Germans advance on Petrograd.

**24 OCTOBER-12 NOVEMBER 1917**
Italians defeated at Caporetto.

**NOVEMBER 1917**
Communist revolution in Russia.
Clemenceau becomes prime minister of France.

**DECEMBER 1917**
British take Jerusalem.

## 1918
Civil War in Russia (to 1921).

## JANUARY 1918
Wilson puts forward his Fourteen Points.

## 3 MARCH 1918
Germany and Russia sign Treaty of Brest-Litovsk (right).

## 21 MARCH-5 APRIL 1918
Ludendorff offensive on Somme. Foch appointed to be supreme commander of Allied forces.

## 9-29 APRIL 1918
Ludendorff's Lys offensive.

## 27 MAY-2 JUNE 1918
Ludendorff's offensive on River Aisne.

## 28 MAY 1918
US forces see action at Cantigny.

## 9-13 JUNE 1918
Ludendorff's offensive on the River Oise.

## 15 JULY-5 AUGUST 1918
Ludendorff's last offensive, on the Marne, met by Foch's counterattack.

## 8 AUGUST-4 SEPTEMBER 1918
Allied Amiens offensive.

## 12-16 SEPTEMBER 1918
US offensive at St Mihiel.

## 26 SEPTEMBER 1918
Allies launch Meuse-Argonne offensive (foot of page).

## 27 SEPTEMBER 1918
Allies launch Cambrai-St. Quentin and Flanders offensives.

## 29 SEPTEMBER 1918
Bulgaria signs an armistice.

## 1 OCTOBER 1918
British take Damascus in Syria.

## 4 OCTOBER 1918
Germans abandon Hindenburg Line.

## 23 OCTOBER-NOVEMBER 1918
Austro-Hungarians overwhelmed on Italian Front.

## 30 OCTOBER 1918
Turkey signs armistice.

## 3 NOVEMBER 1918
Austria-Hungary signs armistice.

## 6 NOVEMBER 1918
Allies take Sedan.

## 11 NOVEMBER 1918
Armistice on Western Front.

## JANUARY 1919
Paris Peace Conference opens at Versailles.

## 28 JUNE 1919
Germany signs Treaty of Versailles.

## 10 SEPTEMBER 1919
Austria signs Treaty of St Germain en Laye.

## 27 NOVEMBER 1919
Bulgaria signs Treaty of Neuilly.

## 4 JUNE 1920
Hungary signs Treaty of Trianon.

## 10 AUGUST 1920
Turkey signs Treaty of Sèvres.

# GLOSSARY

**abdicate** To step down as a monarch as a deliberate choice.

**AEF** American Expeditionary Force, the US troops in Europe.

**alliance** An agreement between states for their mutual help in time of war.

**Allies, the** Russia, France, Britain, Belgium, Italy, the USA and the countries that fought with them in World War I.

**ally** A state that has formally agreed to assist another, usually in war.

**annex** To take over.

**ANZAC** Australia and New Zealand Army Corps.

**armistice** Cease-fire.

**arms race** Two or more countries trying to outdo each other by building up their armed forces.

**artillery** Heavy guns.

**assassinate** To murder a well-known figure, usually for political reasons.

**attrition** The wearing down of the enemy.

**Austria-Hungary** Empire of Austria and Hungary, joined in 1867.

**autocratic** All-powerful.

**BEF** British Expeditionary Force, British troops on the Western Front.

**Balkans** Region between the Black Sea and the Adriatic.

**blockade** Cutting off supplies.

**blockhouse** Concrete shelter.

**brigade** Army unit of about 1,000 men.

**bombardment** Continuous heavy artillery attack.

**bureaucracy** Civil service.

**cabinet** Leading members of a government.

**capital** Main city in a country, where government is located.

**casualty** Soldier killed or wounded.

**cavalry** Soldiers who fight on horseback.

**Central Powers** Germany, Austria-Hungary, Turkey and Bulgaria.

**colony** Territory, usually overseas, seized by an empire.

**Communism** System of government which outlaws private ownership of property and seeks to make sure that wealth is distributed equally among all people.

**conference** A high-level meeting.

**Congress** US parliament.

**contingent** Group of soldiers.

**convoy** Many merchant ships travelling together under the escort of warships.

**Cossacks** Tribal cavalrymen from southern Russia.

**coup** Sudden attempt to seize power.

**Dardanelles** The narrow strip of water between the Bosphorus and the Aegean.

**deadlock** When neither side in a conflict is able to make progress.

**depleted** Run down.

**depth charge** Explosive device timed to go off at a pre-set depth to damage a submarine.

**disband** To break up an armed force.

**division** Army unit of about 10,000 men.

**dog-fight** One-to-one combat between fighter aircraft.

**dreadnought** A fast, heavily armoured battleship.

**Eastern Front** Battle front between the Central Powers and Russia.

**empire** Many territories, often in different parts of the world, ruled by the same government.

**engagement** Battle.

**entente** Informal agreement.

**fiasco** Farcical disaster.

**flank** Side.

**front** The place where two opposing forces meet.

**garrison** Troops in a regular base.

**Grand Fleet** Britain's main battle fleet in World War I.

**guerrillas** Irregular soldiers who avoid set-piece conflicts.

**Hindenburg Line** German pre-prepared defensive line on the Western Front.

**High Seas Fleet** Germany's main battle fleet in World War I.

**home front** The lives of civilians of all warring countries, away from the battle front.

**imperial** Belonging to an empire.

**infantry** Foot soldiers.

**military, the** Armed forces.

**mine** Naval bomb, either floating on or under the surface of the sea.

**minister** Person responsible for an area of government, such as war or finance.

**monitor** To keep an eye on.

**morale** The mood or spirit of a people at war.

**munitions** Provisions of war, such as bullets and guns.

**mutiny** To refuse to obey orders or fight.

**neutral** Not taking sides in a conflict.

**no-man's-land** The narrow strip of land between two front lines.

**obsolete** Out of date.

**offensive** A large-scale attack.

**outflank** To go round the side of.

**peninsula** Area of land surrounded on three sides by water.

**prime minister** Leading or chief minister, the head of government.

**province** Part of a country or empire.

**Prussia** Area of Eastern Germany around Berlin.

**radical** Eager for sweeping, deep-seated change.

**reconnaissance** Searching for information about the landscape and any forces on it.

**reinforcements** Extra troops.

**reparations** Compensation payments.

**revolution** A complete, swift and permanent change.

**salient** Bulge in the front line that extends into enemy territory.

**salient-busting** Eliminating bulges in the front line.

**Schlieffen Plan** German war plan, drawn up in 1905 and later modified, to defeat France before Russia.

**sector** Part or section.

**shell** A projectile fired from a gun, containing an explosive charge and/or shrapnel balls propelled by a charge which can either be contained in the shell case, or loaded into the gun separately.

**spotter aircraft** Reconnaissance plane.

**stalemate** Position where no side appears to be able to win, deadlock.

**strategy** Overall war plans.

**theatre of war** Area where fighting takes place.

**torpedo** Self-propelled underwater missile.

**tsar** Russian emperor.

**turbine** Engine driven by fan blades.

**turret** Swivelling armoured gun emplacement on a ship.

**U-boat** German submarine.

**undermanned** Without sufficient people to carry out a plan.

**unrestricted** Unlimited.

**Western Front** Front lines between the Allies and the Central Powers in France and Belgium.

**Zeppelin** German military airship.

# FURTHER INFORMATION

## RECOMMENDED BOOKS

Brendon, Vyvyen *The First World War, 1914-18*, Hodder & Stoughton Educational, 2000.

Brooman, J. *The Great War: The First World War 1914-18*, Longman, 1985.

Grant, Reg *Armistice, 1918*, Hodder Wayland, 2000.

Hansen, Ole Steen *The War in the Trenches*, Hodder Wayland, 2000.

Mair, Craig *Britain at War, 1914-1919*, John Murray, 1989.

Ross, Stewart *Battle of the Somme*, Hodder Wayland, 2003.

Ross, Stewart *Causes of the First World War*, Hodder Wayland, 2002.

Ross, Stewart *Leaders of the First World* War, Hodder Wayland, 2002.

Ross, Stewart *Technology of the First World War*, Hodder Wayland, 2003.

Wrenn, Andrew *The First World War*, CUP, 1997.

## FIRST-HAND ACCOUNTS

Blunden, Edmund *Undertones of War*, London, 1928, and many further editions.

Britten, Vera *Testament of Youth*, Victor Gollancz, 1933.

Graves, Robert *Goodbye to All That*, Cassell, 1929, and many further editions.

Lewis, Cecil *Sagittarius Rising*, Peter Davies, 1936, and many further editions.

Manning, Frederick *The Middle Parts of Fortune*, privately published 1929, then Penguin 1990 and other editions.

Remarque, Erich Maria *All Quiet on the Western Front*, Putnam, 1929, and many further editions.

Sassoon, Siegfried *Memoirs of an Infantry Officer*, Faber, 1930, and many further editions.

For poetry see Jon Silkin, ed., *The Penguin Book of First World War Poetry*, Penguin, 1979.

## SOURCES OF QUOTATIONS

*A Farewell To Arms*, Ernest Hemingway, Arrow edition, 1994.

*All Quiet On the Western Front*, Erich Remarque, Triad Panther edition, 1977.

*Arab-Israeli Conflict and Conciliation: A Documentary History*, edited by Bernard Reich, Praeger, 1995.

*Great Issues in American History: From Reconstruction to the Present Day, 1864-1969*, edited by Richard Hofstadter, Vintage Books, 1969.

*Somme*, Lyn Macdonald, Penguin, 1983.

*The Great War*, edited by H.W. Wilson and J.A. Hammerton, Odhams, 1915.

*The Imperial War Museum Book of the First World War*, edited by Malcolm Brown, Sidgwick and Jackson, 1991.

*They Called it Passchendaele*, Lyn Macdonald, Penguin, 1993.

*Twenty-five Years, 1892-1916*, Viscount E. Grey, Hodder & Stoughton, 1925.

## RECOMMENDED WEBSITES

Among the many:

www.pvhs.chico.k12.ca.us/~bsilva/projects/great_war/causes.htm
www.schoolshistory.org.uk/firstworldwar.htm
www.btinternet.com/~mrfield/SchoolHist/lessons/wwi/objectives_wwi.html
http://mars.acnet.wnec.edu/~grempel/courses/wc2/lectures/worldwar1.htmlwww.lib.msu.edu/sowards/balkan/lect15.htm
www.schoolshistory.org.uk/firstworldwar.htm
www.btinternet.com/~mrfield/SchoolHist/lessons/wwi/objectives_wwi.htm
www.worldwar1.com/bioindex.htm
www.spartacus.schoolnet.co.uk/FWWpolitical.htm

### Note to parents and teachers

Every effort has been made by the publishers to ensure that these websites are suitable for children; that they are of the highest educational value; and that they contain no inappropriate or offensive material. However, because of the nature of the Internet, it is impossible to guarantee that the contents of these sites will not be altered. We strongly advise that Internet access is supervised by a responsible adult.

## PLACES TO VISIT

Imperial War Museum, London.
National Army Museum, London.
The site of the battlefield at Ieper (Ypres) in Belgium.
Battlefields, graveyards and war memorials of France, perhaps starting at Peronne and Albert.

# INDEX

Numbers in **bold** refer to captions to pictures or, where indicated, to maps, or to text panels.

GREAT RELIGIOUS LEADERS

# Moses
## and
# Judaism

Sharon Barron

HODDER
*Wayland*

an imprint of Hodder Children's Books

# Great Religious Leaders

| | |
|---|---|
| The Buddha and Buddhism | Jesus and Christianity |
| Guru Nanak and Sikhism | Muhammad and Islam |
| Krishna and Hinduism | Moses and Judaism |

© White-Thomson Publishing Ltd 2002

Produced for Hodder Wayland by White-Thomson Publishing Ltd
2/3 St Andrew's Place, Lewes, E Sussex, BN7 1UP, UK

Editor: Margot Richardson          Graphics and maps: Tim Mayer
Designer: Jane Hawkins             Proofreader: Philippa Smith

First published in 2002 by Hodder Wayland, an imprint of Hodder Children's Books

The right of Sharon Barron to be identified as the author of this Work has been asserted by her in accordance with the Copyright, Designs and Patents Act 1988.

All rights reserved. No part of this publication may be reproduced, stored in a retrieval system, or transmitted, in any form or by any means without the prior written permission of the publisher, nor be otherwise circulated in any form of binding or cover other than that in which it is published and without a similar condition being imposed on the subsequent purchaser.

A catalogue record for this book is available from the British Library.
Barron, Sharon
    Moses and Judaism. - (Great Religious Leaders)
    1. Moses (Prophet) 2. Judaism - Juvenile literature  I. Title
    296
ISBN  0 7502 3704 X

Printed in Hong Kong

Hodder Children's Books
A division of Hodder Headline Ltd
338 Euston Road, London NW1 3BH

Cover top: Moses descending from Mount Sinai, carrying the tablets of stone.
Cover main: Orthodox Jews with the Torah at the Western Wall, Jerusalem.
Title page: Orthodox Jews at a bar mitzvah at the Western Wall, Jerusalem.

| SANDWELL LIBRARY & INFORMATION SERVICE | |
|---|---|
| I1730595 | |
| Cypher | 15.05.02 |
| J296 | £11.99 |
| | |

Picture Acknowledgements: The publisher would like to thank the following for permission to reproduce their pictures:
AKG 7 (Erich Lessing), 8 (Cameraphoto), 9, 10, 11 both, 12, 13, 14, 15, 16, 18, 22, 23, 33, Art Directors and Trip Photo Library 5 (A Tovy), 26 (H Rogers), 27 (top) (H Rogers), 27 bottom (I Genut), 30 (I Genut), 31 (J Greenberg), 32 (K McLaren), 36 (top) (J Greenberg), 36 (bottom) (I Genut), 43 (A Tovy), 45 (A Tovy); James Davis Photography 29; Paul Doyle title page; Eye Ubiquitous 20 (David Peez), 42 (Chris Fairclough); Sonia Halliday 34 (David Silverman), 38 (both) (David Silverman), 29 (David Silverman); Impact 24 (Rachel Morton), 28 (Simon Shepheard); Christine Osborne 7 (top), 19 (Ann Cook), 25, 40; Panos Pictures 44 (N. Durrell-McKenna); David Silverman 35, 41; Stockmarket 37, 40; Hodder Wayland Picture Library 6, 17 (Rupert Horrox).

# Contents

# What is Judaism?

Judaism is the religion of the Jewish people. The story of how it began is told in the early books of the Bible, which Jews call the Torah.

## Early Judaism

The founding father of Judaism was Abraham, who lived approximately 4,000 years ago. Although he lived amongst people who worshipped many gods, Abraham believed that there was just one God. He was able to recognize God's voice and trusted Him when God told him to leave his home and go to a place called Canaan. God rewarded Abraham for his faith. He promised Abraham that he would become the father of a great nation and that he and his descendants would hold the land of Canaan for ever. Canaan became known as 'the Promised Land' and is in roughly the same area as present-day Israel.

The map below shows Canaan; the area in Egypt where the Israelites settled; and the route they took when they left Egypt to travel back to the Promised Land. ▼

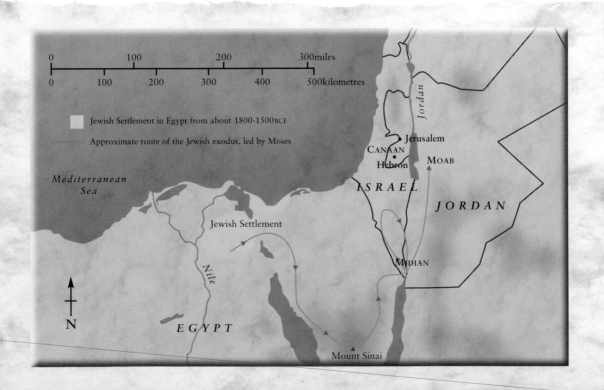

0   100   200   300miles
0   100   200   300   400   500kilometres

Jewish Settlement in Egypt from about 1800-1500BCE

Approximate route of the Jewish exodus, led by Moses

Mediterranean Sea

Jordan

Jerusalem
CANAAN
Hebron   MOAB

ISRAEL

JORDAN

Jewish Settlement

Nile

MIDIAN

N

EGYPT

Mount Sinai

The early Jews, who were called Hebrews, or later, Israelites, remained in Canaan for about 200 years, until a terrible famine forced them to leave. They travelled to Egypt, where food was more plentiful. At first they prospered in Egypt, but their good fortune did not last. An Egyptian ruler, called a pharaoh, made them slaves. They were slaves in Egypt for over 200 years, until God took pity on them and sent Moses to lead them to freedom.

## What do Jews believe?

Jews believe that there is one all-powerful and unchanging God who is the creator of the universe.

Every morning and evening observant Jews will recite a special prayer called the *Shema*. If it is at all possible, they also recite the *Shema* before they die. The *Shema* sets out the most important Jewish beliefs and responsibilities. It reminds Jews of their duty to love God and to obey His commandments. They should take especial care to teach these to their children. The *Shema* ends by saying that it was God who rescued the Jews from slavery in Egypt.

▲ A traditional Jewish family at the Western Wall in Jerusalem (see page 30).

### THE BEGINNING OF THE SHEMA

'Hear, O Israel! The LORD is our God, the LORD is one. You shall love the LORD your God with all your heart and with all your soul and with all your might. Take to heart these instructions with which I charge you this day. Impress them upon your children. Recite them when you are at home and when you are away, when you lie down and when you get up.'

Deuteronomy 6: 4–8

# The Life of Moses

### The Israelite baby

The Israelites became slaves in Egypt because a new pharaoh did not trust them. He thought that there were too many of them and worried that they might make trouble for him. So he made them work as slaves. Their work was back-breaking and life was very cruel.

▲ The Israelites suffered greatly when they were slaves in Egypt.

However, the Pharaoh was not yet satisfied. He ordered that all the Israelite baby boys should be killed as soon as they were born. Every Jewish mother prayed that she would give birth to a girl. The Pharaoh ordered all Egyptians to look for Israelite baby boys and throw them straight into the River Nile.

One mother decided that she must save her baby. She had managed to keep him hidden for three months, but was scared that he would be discovered. So, in desperation, she found a basket and smothered it in tar to make it watertight. She put her baby into the basket and hid it amongst the reeds that grew along the riverbank. She sent Miriam, her daughter, to watch over the baby from a distance.

The Pharaoh's daughter liked to bathe in the river and that day she passed the very spot where the baby was hidden. She noticed the basket and sent one of her slave girls to fetch it. When she looked inside she saw the most beautiful baby she had ever seen. She realized that he was an Israelite baby, but when he started to cry she knew that she could not let him come to any harm.

Miriam approached the princess nervously, 'If you are going to keep this baby, I could find you a good nurse,' she offered. She ran home for her mother. So the Egyptian princess adopted Moses, and his real mother became his nurse.

An ancient Jewish tale says that God sent a plague of searing heat to Egypt which affected the princess very badly. However, as soon as she touched the infant Moses her ills miraculously disappeared. ▶

▲ An ancient wall painting shows us how the princess might have looked.

## THE EGYPTIAN PRINCESS

We know little about the Egyptian princess except that she was a kind-hearted woman who saved the baby. She must have been very brave to challenge Pharaoh's orders. In the Bible we are told that her name was Bithia. This means 'Daughter of God', a suitable name for someone who acted so well. She called her adopted son Moses. The name comes from Egyptian and Hebrew words that mean 'to draw out'. Bithia chose it because she drew Moses out of the river.

## The burning bush

Moses grew up in the royal court and became a prince of Egypt. However one day he noticed an Egyptian beating an Israelite slave. Moses was so angry he killed the Egyptian man. Moses was now in great trouble and was a wanted man.

Moses fled to Midian, outside Egypt, only to become involved in more trouble. A group of men had attacked some girls who were tending a flock of sheep. Moses rescued them and was welcomed by their grateful family. He married one of the girls and settled in Midian. He was no longer a prince. Moses had become a humble shepherd and was very happy in his new life.

▲ This ancient mosaic from Italy shows Moses staring in amazement at the burning bush.

One day, while out with the sheep, Moses saw an incredible sight. There, on the open ground, miles from anywhere, he saw a burning bush. It blazed furiously but remained undamaged. Moses could not believe what he was seeing. A voice called to him from the bush and announced itself as the voice of God. Moses listened in absolute amazement as God instructed him to return to Egypt. He told Moses to tell Pharaoh to free the slaves and to tell them that he was going to lead them out of Egypt and into the Promised Land.

Moses was horrified. 'No one will take any notice of me. Pharaoh won't let the slaves go and none of them will believe that I am telling them the truth!' he cried.

'Moses, what is in your hand?' asked God. Moses jumped back as the shepherd's crook that he had been holding changed into a slithering snake. 'Catch hold of it, Moses, and see what happens.' Moses grasped the snake by its tail and once again it was his shepherd's crook. 'With this and other signs that I shall give you, you will be able to convince them all,' said God.

But Moses was still unsure. 'How can I?' he protested. 'I get nervous and stutter when I have to speak to people.'

God was getting more than a little angry with him. 'I will send your brother, Aaron, with you as your spokesperson. That is enough now, Moses, the matter is settled.'

▲ These illustrations come from a fourteenth-century Hagadah (see page 40). They show Moses at the burning bush (top left); his reunion with his brother, Aaron (top right); the two brothers meeting Pharaoh (bottom left); and trying to impress him with the magical powers given to them by God (bottom right).

### A LEGEND ABOUT MOSES

Moses spent a long time chasing a stray lamb. He caught up with it when it stopped to drink from a stream. Moses said how sorry he was that he had not realized the lamb had been thirsty. He saw that the lamb was tired and carried it all the way back to the flock. God noticed Moses' kindness and the care he had taken over one stray lamb. He decided Moses was just the man to shepherd his own flock, the people of Israel.

### Let my people go!

Moses and Aaron met Pharaoh to ask for the slaves' release, but Pharaoh just laughed at them and ordered the slaves to work even harder.

Moses and Aaron went to Pharaoh again. They tried to dazzle him with the magic shepherd's crook, but he was not impressed. Their next meeting took place on the bank of the River Nile. Aaron held the crook over the water and the river turned to blood. But Pharaoh's magicians were ready to match Moses and Aaron, trick for trick. They had to try again.

▲ God did not want Pharaoh to give in too easily. This allowed God to show his awesome powers by inflicting ten devastating plagues. These pictures come from an eighteenth-century German Hagadah.

The Israelites were told to slaughter a lamb, mark their doorposts with its blood and to roast and eat the meat. This night gave rise to the festival of Pesach (see pages 38–41).

God sent a plague of frogs to Egypt and Pharaoh seemed about to give in, but at the very last minute he changed his mind. God then sent a plague of lice. Pharaoh became more and more angry, but he would not give in. Swarms of insects followed the lice. A terrible disease killed off all the Egyptian livestock, but still Pharaoh would not free the slaves. God told Moses to throw handfuls of soot into the air. The dust from the soot settled all over the country and spread a plague of festering boils. Next came a shower of enormous hailstones that ruined Egypt's crops. The Egyptian people begged Pharaoh to give in. He refused, and swarms of locusts finished off any crops that the hail had missed. Then came three days and nights of total darkness. It seemed that nothing would weaken Pharaoh's will.

God told Moses to prepare the Israelites to move quickly. Moses ordered each family to slaughter a lamb and mark their doorposts with the lamb's blood. Behind the marked doors they were safe, but that night all first-born Egyptian sons died, and a grieving Pharaoh finally agreed to let the slaves leave.

Moses and the Israelites fled to the Sea of Reeds. Looking back, they saw that Pharaoh had changed his mind yet again and that the Egyptians were chasing them. God ordered Moses to hold his arm out over the sea and the waters parted miraculously to allow the Israelites to cross safely. The Egyptians attempted to follow. At a signal from Moses, the sea returned to normal and all the Egyptians were drowned.

## In the wilderness

After crossing the Sea of Reeds, Moses and the Israelites travelled into the desert. After seven weeks, they arrived at the foot of Mount Sinai. God had summoned Moses to the mountain to receive the Ten Commandments on tablets of stone. Moses was away with God for forty days and forty nights and the people became tired and anxious. Moses had left Aaron in charge but he was not having an easy time. The people had begun to doubt that Moses would ever return.

Aaron was worried. He knew he had to do something to calm the people down. He wanted to give them something they could see, to give them faith. After much thought he told the people to gather together all the gold jewellery that they could find. They came back with the precious metal and Aaron had it melted down. He moulded it into a gleaming, golden statue in the shape of a calf. The people forgot all about God and Moses because they believed Moses had abandoned them. Even though there was no logic to it, they decided to believe that the statue of the golden calf had rescued them from Egypt.

Aaron built an altar in front of the golden calf so that the Israelites could worship the statue. The following day they had a celebration meal with singing and dancing. ▼

God could see all this.
He raged at Moses that
He would destroy these
ungrateful people, but
relented after Moses pleaded
for them. He sent Moses
back with the commandments
written on tablets of stone.

When Moses saw the statue
he became furious. He took
the tablets of stone and
hurled them to the ground.
He ran at the calf and broke
it into a million pieces. He
ground the pieces into
powder, mixed them with
water and made the faithless Israelites drink it.
He dealt very harshly with all those who did not
immediately repent. Some of the people had not
taken part in the calf worship. Moses ordered
them to kill all those who had worshipped the idol.

▲ Even though Moses had
pleaded with God not to destroy
the Israelites, about 3,000
people were killed because of
their lack of faith.

### AARON

Aaron was Moses' elder brother. He became the first High Priest of
Israel and the founder of the priesthood. He has become known as a
peace-loving man and this may be why he gave in to the people and
built the golden calf. Perhaps he believed that the project would
stop the people from fighting each other, or that if sin
took place, he – not the people – would be blamed.
Aaron was much loved. When he died 'All the house
of Israel bewailed Aaron thirty days'. He died before
reaching the Promised Land.

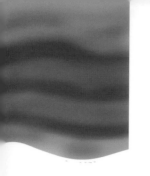

# Moses the Leader, and his Teaching

## What do we know about Moses?

Moses was brought up as an Egyptian prince, but we are told in the Torah that he was a very humble man. He had a stutter and was embarrassed to speak in public. He became a caring shepherd and he would help immediately if he saw that someone was being badly treated.

Moses sometimes had a quick temper. When the Israelites were trekking through the desert, they needed fresh water desperately. God told Moses to gather the people together by a rock and to ask it for water. Instead of asking as he had been told, the anxious and angry Moses hit the rock twice with his staff. God punished Moses severely for his disobedience and for his lack of faith: Moses never got to step inside the Promised Land.

▲ By striking the rock, Moses made it look as though he had produced the water. Instead, he should have shown the people that this power came from God.

Moses was not a God-like figure. He was a man who took on extraordinary tasks and managed to do extraordinary things, but he made mistakes and he had to pay for them. At the very end of his life Moses was allowed to look over into the Promised Land, but he was not allowed to enter.

This illustration shows Moses and Aaron promising food to the hungry Israelites. It comes from a fourteenth-century French Bible. In this illustration, as in many others, Moses appears to have horns. This is entirely due to a mistake in the earliest translation of the Hebrew Bible into Latin. When Moses came down from Mount Sinai, he should have been described as radiant. The mistake in translation implied that he had grown horns.

## Moses and God

When God first called Moses he was afraid and hid his face. However, he recovered quickly and was able to voice his doubts about the mission to Egypt. When his first meeting with Pharaoh was unsuccessful, Moses complained to God that He had broken his promise to deliver the Israelites from slavery. When God threatened to destroy the people after they had built the golden calf, Moses pleaded with him to change his mind.

## How do Jewish people regard Moses?

Moses remains very special to Jewish people. They respect Moses because he was chosen by God to help them. Jewish people call Moses *Moshe Rabbenu*, which means 'Moses, our teacher'. This is because he brought the Torah from God and taught it to the waiting Israelites.

'Never again did there arise in Israel a prophet like Moses – whom the Lord singled out, face to face, for the various signs and portents that the Lord sent him to display in the land of Egypt, against Pharaoh and all his courtiers and his whole country, and for all the great might and awesome power that Moses displayed before all Israel.'

Deuteronomy 34: 10–12

▲ Of all the prophets, it was Moses who was given the ultimate privilege of receiving God's laws on the tablets of stone.

# Moses the leader

## Moses the prophet

Moses was one of many Jewish prophets. These were men and women chosen by God to speak for Him to try to persuade people to mend their ways.

All the prophets were good people, but Moses was special and was the most favoured by God. When Moses' brother and sister, Aaron and Miriam, criticized him, God reminded them how very special Moses was:

> 'Hear these My words: When a prophet of the LORD arises among you, I make myself known to him in a vision, I speak with him in a dream. Not so with My servant Moses: he is trusted throughout My household. With him I speak mouth to mouth, plainly and not in riddles, and he beholds the likeness of the LORD.'

Numbers 12: 6–8

## The covenant

Moses was the link between God and the Israelite people. When God gave Moses the Ten Commandments on Mount Sinai, He made an agreement with Moses as the representative of the Jewish people. This agreement, known as a covenant, was made with all Jewish people, not just with those

◀ The Jewish people keep the covenant alive today by obeying God's commandments. This family are keeping the commandment to remember the Sabbath day by walking to the synagogue for the morning service.

'Now then, if you will obey Me faithfully and keep My covenant, you shall be My treasured possession among all the peoples ... you shall be to Me a kingdom of priests and a holy nation.'

Exodus 19: 5–6

who were present at Mount Sinai at that time, but with all those from the generations to follow.

As His part of the agreement, God promised to take care of the Jewish people. In return the Jewish people had to promise that they would obey God's commandments. Jews are sometimes called the Chosen People. The Jews were not chosen by God because they were a large or powerful nation. They were chosen because they were willing to follow God's laws.

# Moses, the teacher

## The Ten Commandments

Seven weeks after they had fled from Egypt, God ordered Moses to tell the people to get ready, because he wanted to speak to them. Three days later they saw that Mount Sinai was covered by thick smoke. The mountain trembled. There were great bursts of thunder and lightning and the constant blaring of air blown through a ram's horn. This dramatic build-up highlights the importance of what was to come.

God called Moses to the top of the mountain and gave him the Ten Commandments. These orders, taken by Moses to the waiting Israelites, became the starting point for the whole of Jewish law and for legal systems all over the world.

### THE TEN COMMANDMENTS

1. I am the Lord your God who brought you out of the land of Egypt.
2. You shall have no other gods beside Me.
3. You shall not swear falsely by the name of the Lord your God.
4. Remember the Sabbath day and keep it holy.
5. Honour your father and your mother.
6. You shall not murder.
7. You shall not commit adultery.
8. You shall not steal.
9. You shall not bear false witness against your neighbour.
10. You shall not covet your neighbour's house or anything that is your neighbour's.

Exodus 20: 2–14

▲ When God handed Moses the tablets of the law, He told him they were to be stored in an 'Ark' made from wood and gold.

## The 613 *mitzvot*

Although there were ten main commandments, 613 commandments were given altogether. In Hebrew, the commandments are called *mitzvot*.

There are many *mitzvot* about food and its preparation. They detail which foods Jews may eat (kosher) and those that are not allowed. Another group of *mitzvot* deals with *tzedaka*: how Jews should help those in need. Helping others plays a large part in the life of any Jewish community.

Orthodox Jews follow the *mitzvot* as they are written and believe that doing this will strengthen their connection to God. They believe that the *mitzvot* are written in the words of God and must not be altered.

Modern followers of Judaism think that the *mitzvot* were written by men who were inspired by God. But, because they do not accept that the *mitzvot* are written in the actual words of God, they believe that they can be reinterpreted and adapted to a modern way of life.

▲ Hasidic Jews in Jerusalem, Israel. The Hasidic movement began in Poland in the eighteenth century and its members are ultra orthodox. They continue to dress in the Eastern European costume of their original leaders.

# The Sacred Texts

## The Tenakh

The Jewish Bible is called the *Tenakh*, and it has three parts: the Torah (the Five Books of Moses); *Nevi'im* (the books of the Prophets) and *Ketuvim* (the Writings).

The *Tenakh* gets its name from the first letters of the title of each of the three sections: TNK. The *Tenakh* is sometimes called the Written Law.

### The Torah

The Five Books of Moses are the most important books of the *Tenakh* because they contain the laws of Judaism and because they tell the story of how Judaism began.

The book of Genesis is about the creation of the world, Noah's flood and the lives of the Patriarchs: Abraham, Isaac and Jacob. Exodus tells how God guided Moses to rescue the people of Israel from Egypt and how they received God's holy law. Leviticus outlines many of the laws. In Numbers, Moses deals with uprisings and wars and sets up a council of elders to help him lead the people.

◀ The Torah is so important it is treated with great reverence.

The last of the five books, Deuteronomy, is Moses' farewell to the people. Before his death, Moses repeats the laws and teaching revealed in the first four books.

## The Torah and the Bible

The Five Books of Moses are also part of the first section of the Bible which is called the Old Testament. Jewish people do not use the term Old Testament because the second part of the Bible, the New Testament, is not part of Jewish scripture.

This father is teaching his son to read the Torah from a printed version called a Chumash. People use a Chumash for study purposes and for following the Torah reading in the synagogue. ▼

### READING THE TORAH

The Five Books of Moses have been divided into fifty-four sections. Each of these sections is called a *sidra*. A *sidra* is read each week at the synagogue, during the Shabbat morning service and on Monday and Thursday mornings. In the course of a year each of the fifty-four sections will have been read.

Although Jewish people speak of 'reading' from the Torah, the *sidra* is actually chanted rather than read. When the passage is finished, the Torah scroll is lifted up and the congregation says: 'And this is the Torah, which Moses set before the children of Israel, according to the commandment of the Lord by the hand of Moses.'

## *Nevi'im* (Prophets)

The story of the Jewish people is continued in the books of the Early Prophets. After the death of Moses, Joshua (Moses' assistant) led the Jewish people across the River Jordan into Canaan, the Promised Land. A monarchy was set up and the people were ruled by three powerful kings: Saul, David and Solomon. After Solomon's death, the country was divided into the kingdoms of Judah and Israel.

The first book of the Later Prophets is the Book of Isaiah. This contains the famous prophecy of Isaiah: that one day everyone will live in peace and harmony and there will be no more war.

▲ Before Moses died, he asked God to appoint a new leader. God instructed him to find Joshua and place his hand upon him. This action showed the transfer of leadership from Moses to Joshua.

A passage from Prophets, called the *haftarah*, is read aloud in the synagogue after the reading of the *sidra*.

## Ketuvim

*Ketuvim* means 'the writings' and it is a collection of fourteen different books. *Ketuvim* begins with the Book of Psalms. The Book of Psalms is a series of songs written in praise of God. There are 150 psalms in all, and it is thought that almost half of them could have been written by King David. Moses himself might even have written Psalm 90, which is headed 'A prayer of Moses, the man of God.' Psalms play an important part in synagogue services.

Many of the other books of *Ketuvim* continue the history of the Jews. Some of these books are read in the synagogue on specific festivals. The Book of Esther, the story of a brave Jewess who became a queen of Persia, is read on the festival of Purim.

When people tell the story of Jonah, they usually say that he was swallowed by a 'whale'. The Bible actually says that Jonah was swallowed by a big fish. ▼

### PROPHETS

God chose many men and women to become prophets and speak to the people on his behalf. This was not always an easy or a comfortable thing to do. A man called Jonah did not want to be a prophet at all. He ran away from the responsibility and was caught in a terrible storm at sea, thrown overboard and swallowed, as the story goes, by a whale. Eventually he came safely to the shore and carried out the task that God had set him. He went to the city of Nineveh and persuaded the people there to pray that God would forgive their wickedness.

# The writings of the rabbis

## The Talmud

The Talmud is a record of the studies of the early rabbis, who discussed how God's holy laws should be followed. The Talmud has two parts: the Mishnah and the Gemara.

## The Mishnah and the Gemara

Mishnah means 'to learn or to teach by repetition'. The Mishnah was put together by Rabbi Judah the Prince at the beginning of the third century CE. Jews were being forced from their homeland in large numbers and Rabbi Judah recorded the discussions and rulings of the rabbis

### THE RABBI

Rabbi means 'my master' or 'my teacher'. The title of rabbi used to be given to anyone who knew a lot about Jewish law. Today a rabbi has to complete an official course of study. Rabbis still spend a lot of time teaching and explaining points of Jewish law. They may lead the synagogue service, or a cantor or member of the congregation may do it. Women are able to become rabbis of non-Orthodox communities.

This rabbi works in a Reform (non-Orthodox) congregation. She carries out exactly the same duties as her male colleagues. There are no women rabbis in Orthodox Judaism. ▶

so that the all Jews, wherever they lived, would follow the same traditions. The Mishnah covers the whole of Jewish law, from laws about land and crops to those that deal with cleanliness and the burial of the dead. The Gemara is a detailed discussion of the Mishnah.

## The Midrash

The Midrash is a collection of writings by rabbis, many of them stories, that explain something in the *Tenakh*. This could be an event or a commandment. The word midrash means 'enquiry'. A famous midrash explains how Moses got his stutter.

When Moses was a small boy his loyalty was tested by Pharaoh. A precious jewel and a pan of hot coals were placed together on a table and Moses was led towards them. Pharaoh's advisors had told him that if Moses took the jewel, it would mean that one day he would try to take Pharaoh's throne. It would prove that Moses was not to be trusted and that he should be killed. Moses started to reach for the jewel, but an angel nudged his hand towards the pan of coals. Moses picked up a hot coal, touched his mouth with it, burnt his lips and tongue and became 'slow of speech and slow of tongue'.

▲ Wherever they are, Jewish people will gather to study. This study session took place in Warsaw, Poland, during the Second World War. Early in the war the Nazis herded 500,000 Jews into a ghetto and imprisoned them behind a high brick wall. Even as many were dying from starvation or diseases, religious study still took place.

# Parchment scrolls

## Sefer Torah

In synagogues, the Torah is read from a scroll called the Sefer Torah. The Five Books of Moses that make up the Torah are the holiest of all Jewish scriptures and a Sefer Torah is always treated with great care and respect. The Sefer Torah will have a beautiful velvet or wooden cover and other rich ornaments.

A Torah scroll is made from pieces of parchment that have been sewn together to form a single scroll that is about 60 metres long. This long scroll is wrapped around wooden poles that have been attached to each end. The poles are used to unwind the scroll as it is being read. Whilst he or she is reading from the Torah, the reader will point to the words with a finger-shaped pointer called a *yad*. This is so the scroll is not touched unnecessarily.

The Torah is hand-written on the scroll in 250 vertical columns. This is slow and careful work and a scroll will probably take as long as a year to make.

▲ The Sefer Torah is the most sacred of all Jewish objects. When the writing on the scroll has faded so much that it can no longer be read, the scroll is buried with great respect.

The scrolls are kept in the synagogue, in a special cupboard called the Ark. The congregation stands as a mark of respect whenever the Sefer Torah is taken from the Ark.

## Mezuzah

Mezuzah is the Hebrew word for doorpost. It is the name given to a small piece of parchment that has the first two paragraphs of the *Shema* written on it (see page 5). This piece of parchment is rolled into a small, decorative container and fixed to the right-hand doorposts of rooms in a Jewish home. It is a constant reminder of God's presence and commandments.

## Tefillin

Like the mezuzah, tefillin remind the wearer of God's commandments. Tefillin are two small black leather boxes with straps. The first two paragraphs of the *Shema* and two passages from Exodus are written on parchment scrolls in each of the boxes. Orthodox Jewish men wear tefillin while reciting their morning prayers. One of the boxes is worn on the centre of his forehead and the other on his left arm.

▲ The mezuzah is placed in its case and fixed in the upper third of a doorpost.

▼ A Jewish boy will start to use tefillin during morning prayer after he has had his bar mitzvah (see pages 36–7). Tefillin are not used on Shabbat and festivals because it is thought that no further reminder of the covenant is needed.

# Sacred and Special Places

## The Promised Land and the holy city

The land of Israel has been at the heart of Judaism since the religion began. God promised Abraham the land of Canaan for himself and his descendants. Moses led the children of Israel back towards this Promised Land after the hardship of their time as slaves in Egypt.

▲ Much of Israel's fertile land is now used to grow many different kinds of fruit.

### THE PROMISED LAND

'For the LORD your God is bringing you into a good land, a land with streams and springs and fountains issuing from plain and hill: a land of wheat and barley, of vines, figs and pomegranates, a land of olive trees and honey: a land where you may eat food without stint, where you will lack nothing...'

Deuteronomy 8: 7–8

### The land of Israel

Jewish people have not always had control over the land that is now called Israel and for much of their history many Jews have lived outside Israel. But Jewish writings and prayers show that they never forgot their Promised Land and always longed to return. Each time that Orthodox Jews recite a special prayer after they have eaten, they say: 'And rebuild Jerusalem the holy city, speedily and in our day.'

### Jerusalem

The holy city of Jerusalem was built on the site of a fortress captured by King David and is sometimes called the 'City of David'. David's son, Solomon, carried out his father's plan to build a temple there and made Jerusalem the capital of his kingdom. This temple (the First Temple) was destroyed in about 586BCE and the

Jews were forced into exile in Babylon. The Temple was later rebuilt (the Second Temple) and destroyed again, this time by the Romans in 70CE. Jews were expected to travel to Jerusalem three times a year to celebrate the festivals of Pesach, Shavuot and Sukkot while the Temple was still standing. These three festivals are called Pilgrim Festivals. Jerusalem has very special importance for Christians and Muslims as well as for Jews. Pilgrims of all these faiths travel to Jerusalem to visit their holy places.

Sacred Jewish, Muslim and Christian buildings contribute to the special beauty of Jerusalem. The rabbis say that ten measures of beauty came into the world and that, of these ten, Jerusalem took nine. ▼

# Jewish pilgrimage sites in Israel

## The Western Wall

All that remains of the First and Second Temples in Jerusalem today is a part of the wall that was built around the Temple Mount in the first century BCE. This is the most sacred Jewish site. For many centuries Jewish people have come to the Wall to mourn the loss of the Temple and, because of the sound of their crying, it is sometimes called the Wailing Wall.

Today a space has been cleared in front of the Wall for religious services. Bar and bat mitzvah ceremonies are often held there (see pages 36–7).

Visitors often write prayers on pieces of paper and push them between the gaps in the stones, in the hope that prayers sent from such a holy place will be answered favourably.

These boys are being taken to the Western Wall as part of their preparation for bar mitzvah (see page 36). ▼

## Burial sites

There are many sacred burial sites in Israel and the surrounding area. The oldest and largest Jewish cemetery in the world is on the Mount of Olives in Jerusalem. Jews have been buried here for more than 2,000 years. This cemetery is the holiest of all burial sites for Jews.

The Tomb of King David is also in Jerusalem. It was built in the Middle Ages and it is unlikely that it marks David's real burial place, but it has become a site of pilgrimage and prayer. The Patriarchs, Abraham, Isaac and Jacob, are thought to have been buried at the Cave of Machpelah in Hebron.

These sites, as well as the graves of many famous rabbis, are holy places where people come to pray to God. They sometimes leave written prayers at these holy places as they do at the Western Wall.

▲ The Mount of Olives used to be covered by olive trees. Instead of flowers, Jewish people place a small stone on a grave as a sign that they have visited.

### THE DEATH OF MOSES

Rabbinical legend says that as Moses died he was kissed by God. Moses has no known burial place.

'So Moses the servant of the LORD died there in the land of Moab, at the command of the LORD. He buried him in the valley of the land of Moab, near Beth-peor; and no one knows his burial place to this day.'

Deuteronomy 34: 5–6

## WHAT WAS THE HOLOCAUST?

In the 1930s the Jews of Germany lost their freedom, just as the Israelites had in Egypt so many years before. But Adolf Hitler, the leader of the German Nazis, attempted to destroy the Jews completely. The Nazis sent Jews from all over Europe to death camps. Six million Jews had been killed by the end of the Second World War. One-and-a-half million of these were children.

◀ The Children's Memorial at Yad Vashem was hollowed out from an underground cavern.

# Places to remember the Holocaust

## Yad Vashem

Yad Vashem is Israel's memorial to those who died in the Holocaust. It is a large complex built on the Mount of Remembrance in Jerusalem with exhibition halls, museums and special collections of art and information about the Holocaust. The names of those who died are displayed here and there is a special and very sad memorial to all the children who died. The memorial candles placed there are reflected in the darkness and look like stars shining in a dark sky.

## The Anne Frank house

Before the Second World War, Anne Frank was a lively Jewish schoolgirl living in Amsterdam. When the Nazis invaded Holland Anne and her family were in great danger. Her father made plans for them to hide in a secret apartment above his office. In 1942, with the help of trusted friends, the Frank family disappeared from view. They remained hidden for two years. They were betrayed in August 1944, captured by the Germans and sent to a death camp. Anne died just two months before the end of the war.

Her father survived and after the war returned to Amsterdam where he found Anne's diary. The diary was published and Anne became famous. Today her hiding place, the Secret Annexe, is a museum. Thousands of people from all over the world, Jewish people especially, visit her former hiding place out of respect for her memory.

## Memorial sites across the world

There are memorials to the Holocaust victims all over the world. The former death camp of Auschwitz-Birkenau (in Poland) has become a museum memorial to those who were murdered there, as have many of the other camps. There is a Holocaust Memorial Museum in Washington, USA, and an underground memorial crypt in Paris. A museum in Copenhagen tells a happier story. It shows how most Danish Jews were helped to escape to safety in Sweden.

▲ Anne's family shared their cramped hiding place with another four people. Otto Frank, Anne's father, was the only one of the eight inhabitants of the Secret Annexe to survive. His younger daughter's diary has been translated into more than fifty languages and is read all over the world.

# Special Occasions and Festivals

Jewish people celebrate many festivals, spread out through the Jewish calendar. The Sabbath, or Shabbat, is a special day that is celebrated every week by Jewish families.

## Shabbat

The Jewish Sabbath is called Shabbat. Shabbat is the only festival or special day mentioned specifically in the Ten Commandments. It is a day that is set apart from the rest of the week. When Jews rest and pray on Shabbat, they remember that God rested on the seventh day after He created the universe. They also remember that they have the freedom to rest on Shabbat because God rescued them from slavery. Shabbat begins just before sunset on a Friday evening and ends at nightfall on the following day.

## Celebrating Shabbat

Friday evening is a time of celebration in a Jewish home. Orthodox Jews will not do anything that could be classed as work during Shabbat, such as switching on electricity or driving a car. Even families who do not follow all the customs will usually treat Friday evening as different and will gather together to enjoy a special meal. In a traditional home, Shabbat begins when the woman of the house lights the Shabbat candles and

◀ The two Shabbat candles represent the two parts of the fourth commandment, to 'remember' the Sabbath day and to 'keep it holy'.

recites the blessing. In a family with children, the father will bless his children, placing his hands over each child's head as he does so. Then it is time for the Kiddush, a blessing recited over a cup of wine, thanking God for the gift of Shabbat. A further blessing is made over two plaited loaves of bread called challah.

Many families attend synagogue services on Shabbat mornings. The high point of the morning service is when the Sefer Torah is taken from the Ark for the reading of the week's *sidra*.

## CHALLAH

Challah is a type of bread, and is always used on Shabbat and festivals. There are two loaves on the table at Shabbat, as a reminder of the Israelites' desert trek. While they were in the desert, God gave them a food called manna, which was like 'a wafer made with honey'. On the sixth day of the week, God sent them a double portion. This gave them enough to eat on the sixth day and on the seventh, which was Shabbat.

The two loaves are held while the blessing is recited. At the end, everyone responds by saying 'Amen'. The bread is then cut and everyone is given a slice. ▶

A bar mitzvah at the Western Wall. The boy has completed his reading and has been lifted on to his father's shoulders as the family sing and dance in celebration.

A boy making a speech at the party that is being held to celebrate his bar mitzvah. He will pay tribute to his parents, grandparents and teachers. ▼

# Rites of Passage

## Bar mitzvah

When a boy reaches the age of thirteen, he will celebrate his bar mitzvah. The ceremony usually takes place on the Shabbat that follows his thirteenth birthday. It marks the fact that, in the eyes of his religion, the boy has become a man. Bar mitzvah means 'son of the commandment' and the boy should now observe all the Jewish laws. He can take his place as an official member of a minyan, the group of ten men who must be gathered before a service can take place. A boy will now wear his tefillin for morning prayers.

During the synagogue service, the bar mitzvah boy will recite a blessing on the Torah. He will go on to read some or all of the *sidra* and sometimes the *haftarah* or other parts of the service as well. He will have studied very hard to get to this point.

A bar mitzvah is a time for great celebration. The proud parents will give a party and the boy will receive many presents. His parents and grandparents will usually try to give gifts that he will keep always: a tallit (prayer shawl), tefillin or his own kiddush cup.

A bat mitzvah ceremony taking place in a non-Orthodox synagogue. It is held in the same way as a bar mitzvah. The girl is wearing a prayer shawl and is reading from a Sefer Torah. ▼

## Bat mitzvah

Bat mitzvah means 'daughter of the commandment'. Bat mitzvah ceremonies take place when a girl is twelve. Twelve has always been the age when a Jewish girl is considered to have reached adulthood, but it has only become usual to mark this with a ceremony in recent years.

A girl will attend special classes for some time before a bat mitzvah and study the *mitzvot* and Jewish history. She will spend a lot of time learning how to run a Jewish home.

There is not really a set pattern to the ceremony, but it will always include the Torah passage that begins 'A woman of worth who can find? For her price is beyond rubies', (Proverbs 31: 10–11), as a reading or a song.

Reform and Progressive branches of Judaism treat boys and girls in exactly the same way and a bat mitzvah ceremony is held during the regular Shabbat morning service in these congregations.

# Festivals

## Pesach

This festival, also called 'Passover', takes place in spring and lasts for eight days. It is the festival of freedom, the time when the Jewish people remember the exodus from Egypt and thank God for releasing them from slavery. As Jewish people celebrate, they should feel as if they themselves had been rescued from Egypt and set free.

## *Hametz*

On the night that Moses lead the Israelites out of Egypt, they made bread for their journey. They had to leave so quickly that there was no time to wait for the bread to rise. Jewish people remember this by avoiding *hametz* (leavened foods) during Pesach. They do not eat anything made from grain products that have risen or fermented and will eat matzah instead of bread at this time. Matzah is a flat, unleavened bread made from special flour and water, rather like a cracker or crispbread.

Matzah dough is baked within 18 minutes to make sure it will not have any time to rise. ▶

▲ Any last crumbs of *hametz* are gathered together and burnt before Pesach. As it burns, the head of the household recites a blessing.

Some utensils can be made kosher for use during Pesach by immersing them completely in boiling water. ▶

## Cleaning for Pesach

Not only do Jewish people avoid eating leavened foods, but they also avoid using anything that might have come into contact with them. Every trace of leavened food has to be removed from the house before Pesach. The house is spring-cleaned very thoroughly. The crockery, cutlery and kitchen equipment that is usually used is put away and sets that are only ever used during Pesach are brought out instead.

## Pesach cookery

Jewish families all have their favourite foods for Pesach. There are many delicious recipes for special cakes and biscuits. Different communities have slightly different customs. Sephardi Jews (Jews from Spain, Portugal and the Arab countries) continue to eat rice during Pesach. They also eat vegetables such as peas or beans that grow in pods. Ashkenazi Jews (Jews from Northern, Central and Eastern Europe) do not eat these foods during Pesach.

### SEARCHING FOR HAMETZ

However careful a family has been to remove all *hametz* from the house, they will search the house again on the evening before Pesach. This search is called *bedikat hametz*. Somebody will hide some pieces of bread around the house before the search begins. The search will not be over until all the pieces have been found. In this way the family can be absolutely sure that they have made a thorough search for every trace of the *hametz*.

## What is Seder?

The Seder is the service and evening meal celebrated at home on the first two nights of Pesach. Seder means 'order' and on Seder nights everything is done in a particular and unchanging order. The service is divided into two parts by a special meal. Families gather together for the Seder and invite guests to join them who would otherwise be alone. Seder involves the whole family and is at the heart of the celebration of Pesach.

## At the table

The Seder service is read from a book called a Hagadah. This means 'telling'. Many are brightly coloured with beautiful illustrations. The youngest child at the table is

Three pieces of matzah are placed on the Seder table. The middle piece is broken into two and half of it is used for the *Afikomen* (see page 41). After the traditional blessing everyone is given some of the top matzah and the remaining middle half to eat. ▼

▲ A Hagadah illustration that goes with a traditional Seder song called 'One Kid'.

given the job of asking four questions about why the Seder night is different from all other nights. The answers to the questions are given in the 'telling' of the story of how Moses was sent by God to lead the Israelites out of slavery in Egypt.

A Seder plate is placed on the table. It has a number of sections for special foods that also help to tell the story. Everyone must taste the *Haroset* (a mixture of apples, nuts, cinnamon and sugar, that is meant to look like the mortar which the Israelite slaves used in building), and the bitter herbs that represent the bitterness of slavery.

▲ In some families everyone will take it in turns to read aloud from the Haġadah.

During the Seder everyone will drink four cups of wine. (Children will have a tiny cup, or wine mixed with water.) Each cup of wine stands for one of the four promises that God made to the Israelites: 'I will free you', 'I will deliver you', 'I will redeem you' and 'I will take you to be my people'. The Seder evening is long, but everyone enjoys the familiar songs that are sung at the end of the meal.

The Seder takes Jews back to a time when they suffered greatly, but by the end of the evening they start to look forward to a time when everyone will enjoy peace and freedom. The Seder celebration ends with the cry 'Next year in Jerusalem!'

### THE AFIKOMEN

*Afikomen* means 'dessert'. It is the last piece of matzah that is eaten at the Seder. It stands for the last, hurried meal that the Israelites ate before they fled from Egypt. During the evening a father hides the *Afikomen* and the children will have to find it after dinner. The Seder cannot be finished until the *Afikomen* has been found and eaten. The finder gets a reward, as do all the other children who joined in the search!

# Shavuot, Sukkot and Simchat Torah

## Shavuot

The two-day festival of Shavuot, 'the Season of the Giving of Our Law', celebrates the giving of the Torah to Moses on Mount Sinai. The Ten Commandments are read in the synagogue on the first day. Shavuot comes seven weeks after Pesach and is sometimes called the 'Feast of Weeks'.

Sukkot is also the autumn harvest festival. The overhanging branches of the sukkah are decorated with autumn fruits, leaves and fragrant plants. These remain in place throughout the festival. ▼

It is also a harvest festival because it marks the beginning of the summer wheat harvest. On Shavuot it has become customary to eat dairy foods, especially cheesecake, to remember the promise of the 'land of milk and honey'.

## Sukkot

Sukkot commemorates the protection of God during the time that the Jewish people were wandering in the desert. Observant families build a sukkah to use during this eight-day festival in memory of the shelters that the Jews had to build in the desert. A sukkah is a shelter or hut, with three or four sides. Its roof is covered with cut branches and left partly open to the sky. The family will eat and even sometimes sleep in the sukkah.

## THE FOUR SPECIES

Four plants are used during prayer on Sukkot: the palm, myrtle, willow and *etrog*. They are known as the Four Species. The palm branch, myrtle and willow are wound together to form a bundle called a *lulav*. This is held in the right hand. An *etrog*, a yellow fruit that is rather like a lemon, is held in the left hand. At set times during the celebration, the *lulav* is waved in all directions to show that God is everywhere and that He showers His blessings from all sides.

▲ To worship during Sukkot, people try hard to find the freshest and most perfect plants available. The *lulav* has to be green, its ribs should still be tight and it must come to a point at the top. The *etrog* must be yellow and its skin should be blemish-free.

## Simchat Torah

On Simchat Torah, 'the Rejoicing of the Law', the annual cycle of Torah readings comes to an end with the last verses of the Book of Deuteronomy. The readings immediately begin again with the first verses of Genesis.

The festival shows the love that Jewish people have for God's law. Simchat Torah is celebrated with all the joy of a wedding and the Torah readers on Simchat Torah are known as Bridegrooms of the Law. The Sefer Torah is carried around the synagogue, and sometimes outdoors, with much singing and dancing.

# Judaism Today

## Where Jews live

There are approximately 15 million Jewish people today. They live in countries all over the world and come from different racial groups. They may be Ashkenazi (from Northern, Central and Eastern Europe), Sephardi (from Spain, Portugal and the Arab countries), Oriental (from ancient communities such as India and Yemen) or Beta Israel (from Ethiopia).

▲ Most of the ancient Jewish community of Ethiopia was rescued from persecution in the later part of the twentieth century.

The Jewish population of Europe fell dramatically during the Holocaust, when one-third of the world's Jewish population was killed, and the largest numbers of Jews now live in the United States and Israel.

### The State of Israel

Jews had prayed for a return to their homeland ever since they were forced to leave it. In the nineteenth century the Zionist movement was formed. Its aim was the re-establishment of a Jewish homeland. The State of Israel was founded in 1948 and, after the horror of the Holocaust, a second exodus began.

Israel's 'Law of Return' gives every Jew the right to live in Israel and to become an Israeli citizen. The most recent group of new citizens has come from the former Soviet Union. Israel today is home to Jews from all over the world: Europe, the United States, the Arab countries, Ethiopia and beyond.

## Jewish religious movements

There are now a number of Jewish religious movements. They fall into two main groups, Orthodox and non-Orthodox. Orthodox Jews follow traditional religious rules and customs. Some Orthodox Jews belong to Hasidic groups that are strictly observant. The Lubavitch group is one of the largest Hasidic groups. Lubavitch Jews run many education programmes and try to encourage other Jews to become more observant.

There are different non-Orthodox movements in different countries. These groups are not quite the same, but, unlike some Orthodox Jews, they all share a belief that Judaism can be adapted to meet the needs of a changing world.

These Orthodox Jewish men are celebrating at the Western Wall. The area near the wall is divided into two sections according to Orthodox tradition, providing a space for women and a separate space for men. ▼

## Moses and Judaism today

The Torah is the heart of Judaism. This is true for all branches of Judaism, Orthodox and non-Orthodox. All that is different is how they understand and explain it.

Moses has a special place in Judaism, because he was its greatest prophet and the very first Torah teacher. When Moses came down from Mount Sinai and told the people about God's commandments he began the traditions of Judaism that have continued for thousands of years to this day.

# Glossary

**Ark** The cupboard in a synagogue in which the Torah scrolls are kept.

**Bar mitzvah** A ceremony that is held to welcome a Jewish boy into the adult community.

**Bat mitzvah** A ceremony that is held to welcome a Jewish girl into the adult community.

**BCE** Before Christian Era.

**Cantor** The person who leads the prayers during a service in a synagogue.

**CE** Christian Era.

**Commandment** A rule or order given by God.

**Covenant** An agreement or contract, as in the agreement between God and the Israelites.

**Exodus** A mass departure of people.

**Ghetto** A part of a town where Jews were forced to live.

**Hagadah** The book read at the Seder. It tells the story of the Jews' escape from slavery in Egypt.

**Hametz** Leavened food forbidden during Pesach.

**Hebrew** The language of the Jewish Bible and the traditional language of Jewish prayer. A modern version of Hebrew is the language of Israel.

**Holocaust** The persecution and mass-murder of the Jews by the Nazis between 1933 and 1945.

**Kiddush** A blessing said over a cup of wine at the start of Shabbat and festival meals.

**Kosher** Food which Jews are allowed to eat.

**Leavened** Food that has fermented and risen.

**Mitzvot** Commandments. Sometimes used to mean 'good deeds'.

**Observant** Observing the rules of a religion.

**Orthodox Judaism** Traditional Judaism.

**Patriarch** The male head of a family or tribe. Abraham, Isaac and Jacob are the Patriarchs of Judaism.

**Pesach** The festival which marks the escape of the Jews from slavery in Egypt.

**Pharaoh** A ruler of Ancient Egypt.

**Pilgrim** Someone who travels to a holy place for religious reasons.

**Plague** A large number of animals or insects, or a serious disease that causes great damage.

**Prophet** Someone who speaks for God and tells people what God wants.

**Purim** The festival that celebrates the time when Queen Esther saved the Jewish people at the time of King Xerxes II of Persia.

**Rabbi** A Jewish religious teacher and leader.

**Reform Judaism** A non-Orthodox Jewish movement that has made changes to old religious laws and customs to fit in with changing times.

**Sefer Torah** A hand-written Torah scroll.

**Shabbat** The Jewish Sabbath. It begins before sunset on Friday and ends at nightfall on Saturday.

**Shema** An important prayer and statement of belief.

**Sidra** A passage from the Torah read in the synagogue on Shabbat mornings.

**Synagogue** A building where Jewish people meet, pray and study.

**Talmud** A collection of commentary and discussion, written by the early rabbis, known as the Oral Law.

**Tefillin** Two leather boxes containing passages from the Torah, which Jewish men wear on their head and upper arm during morning prayer.

**Tenakh** The Jewish Bible.

**Torah** The Five Books of Moses, but can also mean the Jewish Bible or the whole of Jewish law and teaching.

**Yad** A finger-shaped pointer used when reading from a Sefer Torah in a synagogue.

# Further Information

## Books to read

*The Illuminated Haggadah* edited by Michael Shire (Frances Lincoln, 1998)

*Jewish Festivals Cookbook* by Ronne Randall (Hodder Wayland, 2000)

*Judaism* by Arye Forta (Heinemann Educational, 1995)

*Judaism* by Angela Wood (Franklin Watts, 1999)

*Religions of the World: Jewish World* by Douglas Charing (Hodder Wayland, 2001)

*Tanakh: a New Translation of the Holy Scriptures According to the Traditional Hebrew Text* (Jewish Publication Society: Philadelphia, 1985)

*The Torah* by Douglas Charing (Heinemann Educational, 1993)

*What Do We Know About Judaism?* by Doreen Fine (Macdonald Young Books, 1995)

## Websites

*Akhlah*
http://www.akhlah.com/
A site for Jewish children with information about the Torah, festivals, Israel and Hebrew.

*BBC Online: Religion and Ethics: Judaism*
http://www.bbc.co.uk/religion/judaism/judaism.html
A useful reference site.

*Judaism 101*
http://www.jewfaq.org/
An online encyclopaedia of Judaism.

## Places to visit

### UK and Ireland

Most communities are happy to make arrangements for school parties to visit their synagogue. Synagogues will usually be listed in the phone directory. In case of difficulty, and for further information, contact the Board of Deputies of British Jews (020 7543 5400) or the Scottish Council of Jewish Communities (0141 577 8208).

### Museums

Jewish Museum, Albert Street, London NW1 7ND
Manchester Jewish Museum, 190 Cheetham Hill Road, Manchester M8 8LW
The Irish Jewish Museum, 3/4 Walworth Road, South Circular Road, Dublin 8

### Holocaust Education

Beth Shalom Holocaust Centre, Laxton, Newark, Nottinghamshire NG22 OPA

### Outside the UK

All over the world there are museums dedicated to the memory of those who died in the Holocaust and to the study of Judaism and the Jewish people. A very few are listed below.

Israel
  Jerusalem: Yad Vashem and The Israel Museum
  Tel Aviv: The Museum of the Diaspora
Europe
  Amsterdam: The Anne Frank House
USA
  Washington: The United States Holocaust Memorial Museum
  New York: The Jewish Museum and The Museum of Jewish Heritage
Australia
  Sydney: The Sydney Jewish Museum

# Index

The numbers in **bold** refer to photographs and maps, as well as text.